Rapid SharePoint 2013 Collaboration Solution Development and Deployment

Yaroslav Pentsarskyy

Opinions expressed in this book are those of the author only and do not reflect opinions of product vendors or companies the author worked/works for. Information in this book is distributed on an "as-is" basis, without warranty. Although every effort has been made in the preparation of this work, neither the author nor publisher nor any other party affiliated with the production of this book shall have any liability to any person or entity with respect to any loss or damage caused or alleged to be caused directly or indirectly by the information contained in this work.

This book is an independent publication and is not affiliated with, nor has it been authorized, sponsored, or otherwise approved by Microsoft Corporation.

Microsoft, SharePoint, Microsoft Office, and Windows are trademarks of the Microsoft group of companies.

Copyright © 2012 Yaroslav Pentsarskyy

Cover Design by Luis Ponce

All rights reserved.

ISBN: 1481852574

ISBN-13: 978-1481852579

About the author

Yaroslav has been involved in SharePoint solution architecture and implementation since 2003 as well as he's a Microsoft MVP since 2009. Yaroslav frequently presents at local and worldwide tech events as well as online. He is an avid blogger and writer. His blog, *www.sharemuch.com*, offers fresh information and perspective on the latest SharePoint innovation. He has also published several books on SharePoint including, *Top 60 custom solutions built on SharePoint 2013*, *SharePoint 2013 branding in practice*, and *Microsoft SharePoint 2010 and PowerShell 2.0: Expert Cookbook*.

About the reviewers

Colin Phillips

Colin Phillips is a SharePoint consultant and developer with itgroove Professional Services Ltd. He brings over 12 years' experience in information technology and software development, including stints at small and large software firms such as Cognos (now IBM). Colin provides capable and competent expertise on a variety of SharePoint topics such as custom development solutions, business intelligence, workflows, Nintex, branding, page layouts and design, search, infrastructure, and many more. His blog can be found at http://mmman.itgroove.net

Gurinder Singh Mann

Gurinder Singh Mann is a Technical Consultant with Fujitsu Consulting and a SharePoint Microsoft Certified Professional. With a software engineering degree from Simon Fraser University and over 6 years of experience designing, developing, and maintaining mid-to-large scale enterprise solutions, he remains passionate about SharePoint and Web technologies. Ever vigilant to expand his knowledge and network, he can be connected with via gurindersmann@hotmail.com.

Keith Tuomi

Keith Tuomi, is a SharePoint-focused consultant & developer at itgroove Professional Services Ltd. With extensive experience designing, coding, testing and supporting Microsoft technologies, he works consistently to improve his proficiencies in creative technical development and administration. A programmers approach to detail combined with the inspiration of an architect means there is plenty for him to explore in the world of SharePoint. He blogs regularly at http://yalla.itgroove.net.

Paul Keijzers

Paul has been working extensively with SharePoint since early 2001. During this period he had the pleasure to see the evolution of this collaboration platform. During his career he has fulfilled different positions from developer to SharePoint architect. Nowadays he is the proud owner of 2 companies based in Amsterdam/ The Netherlands. (KbWorks & The Question Factory) with a 100 % focus on Microsoft SharePoint and Office365 technology. Paul is a great networker you can follow him on twitter @KbWorks

Rene Modery

Rene is an Office 365 MVP based in Singapore with more than 5 years of experience in implementing SharePoint based intranets in the region Asia Pacific. In his role, he had the opportunity to get to work first-hand with all aspects of SharePoint, be it administration, implementation, development, training, and others. Rene is very enthusiastic about Office 365 and the possibilities it offers to companies of all sizes. He is a regular presenter at the Singapore SharePoint User Group, and shares his knowledge and experiences on his blog and other publications. Rene holds a Masters in Management Information Systems from the University of Mannheim, Germany.

Table of Contents

Who this book is for 1

What to expect from this book 1

What you need for this book 1

How to provide feedback 2

The code and samples 2

The art and business of enterprise collaboration 3

    Information management 4

    Architecture currency 5

    Content accessibility 6

    Where does this take us 7

1 Your environment set up 9

    1.1 Setting up your development environment 10

    1.2 SharePoint Central Administration 12

2 Overview of major collaboration components in SharePoint 2013 13

    2.1 Overview of site templates 14

    2.2 Publishing Portal 15

    2.3 Team Site 27

    2.4 Community Site 36

    2.5 Project Site 44

    2.6 Enterprise WIKI 49

Table of Contents

    2.7 Enterprise Search Center 55

    2.8 Personal Site...59

    2.9 How does it all fit together 64

3 Applying branding to the collaboration components 67

    3.1 Setting up and understanding your development environment........................68

    3.2 The basics: Changing the look and feel of your SharePoint collaboration sites 72

    3.3 Creating a SharePoint 2013 custom look for collaboration sites..........................76

    3.4 Working with a SharePoint 2013 master page...84

    3.5 Applying a new SharePoint collaboration site master page................................93

    3.6 Adding interaction to your site by extending a SharePoint master page 97

    3.7 Applying a custom user interface to a SharePoint collaboration site 103

    3.8 The basics: Changing the look and feel of SharePoint publishing sites.............115

    3.9 Provisioning and applying your own custom page layouts................................119

    3.10 Working with search site master page 128

    3.11 The basics: Changing the look and feel of Personal Site 135

    3.12 Changing the look and feel of Personal Sites for individual users....................146

    3.13 Putting it all together: automated installation of your branding package to multiple environments 151

4 Customizing features of your collaboration solution 157

    4.1 Extending collaboration site templates 158

    4.2 Extending publishing and other site templates 165

    4.3 Provisioning content pages to your site 170

    4.4 Provisioning web parts, views and other content to your pages........................178

    4.5 Creating SharePoint lists and performing content roll up 183

    4.6 Capturing list events and executing custom logic on events triggering 194

    4.7 Debugging your SharePoint solution 197

    4.8 Customizing SharePoint structured and managed navigation..........................202

    4.9 Customizing SharePoint 2013 suite bar menu 214

Table of Contents

4.10 Working with user profiles and user profile properties 219

4.11 Creating custom user profile properties 224

4.12 Using user profile property values in your solution 232

4.13 Creating recurring background running processes using SharePoint timer jobs 237

4.14 Defining content expiration and automating provisioning of out-of-the-box workflows 243

4.15 Getting started with building SharePoint 2013 apps 252

5 Automating the deployment and configuration of your SharePoint solution 259

5.1 Automating SharePoint site provisioning and configuration 260

etc 267

Index 269

Who this book is for

This book is for Solution Architects, intermediate and senior .NET Developers, intermediate SharePoint developers. You won't need prior experience building solutions for SharePoint but it would be a great asset.

What to expect from this book

This book goes beyond just technicalities and how-to you can typically find online; it'll start with the perspective where collaboration solutions are now and how they will evolve. With that perspective in mind, you will learn what out-of-the-box capabilities of SharePoint are out there and how to create customizations to fill gaps. Assuming you have a technology background, you'll learn how to apply concepts and business context to practical features of SharePoint. Although many of the examples can be applied in the general context of building SharePoint solutions, we will focus on collaboration solutions in this book. This book doesn't focus on the hardware and infrastructure configuration; you will be provided with the resources on how to set up your development environment to be able to execute examples from this book.

As things evolve, you might want to keep in touch and follow my blog at *www.sharemuch.com* to get fresh content and update

What you need for this book

To be able to execute example code in this book you will need a system capable of running SharePoint 2013 Server. We recommend using a virtual environment set up locally or in the cloud. Each scenario with additional configuration requirements will either point you to the configuration steps or will explain the set up for you.

How to provide feedback

Each scenario of this book has gone through multiple stages of review to ensure concepts and examples outlined here run flawlessly. However, things happen and you might want to provide constructive feedback to help us create better content in the future. If so, you're welcome to leave a comment on the author's blog: *www.sharemuch.com* under the contact section.

The code and samples

This book comes with quite a lot of code and you'd be better off downloading it rather than typing it all up from the book pages. You can download the code from *www.sharemuch.com* under the download link.

The art and business of enterprise collaboration

Although this book is targeted for solution architects and developers, we have to clear a few things about the business of collaboration solutions, so we're all on the same page and build solutions that get people excited. After all, you don't want to build meaningless solutions, right?

It might sound obvious, but - every solution has to have a purpose which is clear to a project sponsor(s) to support building of the solution. For example, your company might still be using SharePoint 2007 and that seems pretty old and needing a replacement. Well that's logical, but what are the actual reasons to make an upgrade? Are those reasons and changes going to make your end users' lives easier? How much easier and can you measure it? Once you start thinking in terms of measureable impact, you will right away start seeing the picture from the end user's point of view and combined with your technical expertise you'll be creating solutions that are simple and make a significant impact on end users ... because unless you're building a solution for a technical competition, it's got to make a good impact on end users.

Once your solution has a purpose and you know your measurable goals, it's easier to see which SharePoint features you're going to use to achieve your goals.
Further, we'll take a look at what are some of the typical goals of collaboration solutions, whether it's an intranet, an extranet, or a board site it's all about collaboration.

Information management

What's the goal of implementing a collaboration solution? Most of your answers might fall under the categories of:

- to locate information
- to share information
- to facilitate communication between internal and external groups
- to connect employees and partners
- to bring together work tools

Those are all great, but the categories above can have a different meaning to different people; let's pick on a first one – "to locate information". Think about the company you're currently working at … what are the sorts of departments or work groups you have within that organization?

Now, can you achieve the goal of helping end users find the information so everyone's satisfied?

Let's say your answer is "Yes, using search", well, here is one for you, if users always knew what they were looking for and how to find it, they wouldn't need a search tool in the first place; but most don't, so they search with ambiguous keywords hoping for an answer, which they rarely get. Not to say that using search is hopeless, but it shouldn't be your silver bullet.

I see how this can be hard to accept, since there are at least a few Internet search engines which are highly successful in giving people what they're looking for. But your intranet for example isn't exactly the Internet where everyone contributes, and collective searches help rank better results to the top. Another difference between the Internet and your company's search is that usually there are several hundred, if not more, results that answer a single search query; compare that with the intranet search, where users tend to look for something very specific, like that one presentation, a report, or a proposal and nothing else. For example, most users wouldn't consider Bob's blog post on the company's performance an equivalent of an authoritative source for a formal company presentation. Most of us (architects and developers) seem to consciously or subconsciously understand that and that's good … otherwise our intranets would consist of a single search box and a results page.

Architecture currency

Most collaboration portals have a navigation structure helping users to locate information within it, and that's great, since many contributors have learned about classifying information either by folders or by metadata as long as the established classification structure makes sense.

It's also no surprise that there are many ways something can be classified and users can add new categories which may throw off an existing structure, again, leading to difficulty with locating the information. Going back to our intranet search example from above; even if you specify the most precise query, you might get a number of irrelevant results just because someone has entered the wrong metadata on a piece of content.

The main cause behind this is not recognizing that information structure may evolve, staff skills will evolve, business processes will evolve, and your portal is likely to remain the same since the day it was launched.

See, every intranet you have seen designed so far is likely to go though the following stages: engage end users and collect business requirements, adjust requirements to fit platform features, build the solution and deploy the solution.

This is my oversimplified view of the process since there are a variety of other elements that go into larger intranet implementation such as: change management, information management, user interface design, user acceptance testing, training, post deployment support, etc.

To make things even more simple, the whole process starts with gathering user input and finishes with the deployment of the solution within an organization. Any further maintenance of the solution is just needed to ensure the operational state of the solution. It's very unlikely you will be re-structuring sites and libraries every few months while the solution is in production, and for the right reasons ... changing information structure and architecture every few months is not feasible due to the impact on requirements gathering and user training.

So, you're dealing with evolving content, staff skills, business processes and no changes on a solution front, apart from necessary maintenance.
Now, if your solution interface was able to adapt accordingly depending on particular usage scenarios, would that work? Even better, if the interface adapted to each individual

user and they knew all about the pattern according to which the interface will adapt to them.

That's just one of a few examples of how your portal project can be transformed using out-of-the-box and custom features to drive user adoption of your solution.

Content accessibility

Devices have taken over and people need a reasonable way to do business while on the go. I say reasonable because it's unlikely you will achieve a full fidelity experience across all platforms, it's too, well, 'unreasonable' from the investment standpoint.

Now, think about mobility and SharePoint; did I hear you chuckle?

What if I told you that the main challenge around mobile usage of a SharePoint intranet or extranet is directly tied to information architecture?

Mobile devices vary in form factors and some things are just not feasible to cater on certain form factors. As much fun as it may sound, I really don't want to use my phone to write this book. I also don't want to take out my laptop to open an intranet and approve a vacation request workflow or an expense form.

Sounds pretty logical right? Yet, how many applications and add-ins out there try to facilitate mobile functionality for tasks that just aren't meant for mobile?

So once you boil it down to basics and decide what functionality you're going to make mobile friendly, you may come to the conclusion that it's just one or two web parts on a page. Compare that to making the entire site mobile friendly and responsive. Even if you spend months of time and budget making the whole intranet mobile friendly, there will be several users not happy that they can't edit the page on their phone or something similarly unreasonable at that time.

Just as with anything, the mobile experience deserves its own attention and you should be speaking to mobile end uses within an organization when gathering your requirements; don't make arbitrary assumptions.

I'll give you some of the examples of what part of the intranet users would likely want to see on a mobile device:

- status of the information they currently working with
    - document updates and changes
- project or group communication they're working with
    - group announcements, group or project events or tasks
- group contact list

Seems like a small list? It is, and you can certainly add few more items of your own, but the idea is to give your end users information about a small set of content they care about and they can take care of the rest; whether it involves accessing the content on a full fidelity device or not. If you could give your users the ability to get a feed with updates for the intranet items they chose to follow – it'd provide them with more significant value than clicking through pages on a slow mobile connection while waiting for a green light on an intersection.

Where does this take us

Above are just a few very typical scenarios how traditional approaches to intranet design can create issues with your best efforts in making information accessible.

Each scenario of this book will have a bit of a "business" reasoning - before jumping into technical capabilities and customizations it introduces.

The goal is to give you the most knowledge on out-of-the-box and custom features to build the next generation collaboration solution.

CHAPTER 1

Your environment set up

In this chapter:

- Setting up your development environment
- SharePoint Central Administration

Your environment set up

1.1 Setting up your development environment

There is a variety of ways to starting your SharePoint development and setting up your development environment. You can subscribe to a cloud service, such as _CloudShare.com_, and establish your SharePoint 2013 development environment from a template. This is by far the easiest way to get started since you'll have a machine with basic configuration and all of the development tools installed running in minutes.

Another option is to download and set up your development environment on premises according to Microsoft's guide.

In this section we'll go over the set up steps which will allow you to establish SharePoint 2013 standalone development environment. For production environment steps, we recommend you use the best practices outlined in a set of Microsoft guides, search TechNet for *Overview of SharePoint 2013 installation and configuration*.

For your SharePoint 2013 development environment, we recommend a computer with an x64-capable CPU, and 32 GB of RAM. To ensure you can quickly restore your development environment from unintentional or intentional misconfiguration, we recommend using a Microsoft Hyper-V set up. In this case, you would install SharePoint 2013 on a virtual machine, running a Windows Server 2008 Service Pack 2 x64 (or Windows Server 2008 R2 x64) guest operating system or Windows Server 2012.

Assuming you have a set up a guest operating system and SharePoint 2013 installation package, run the **PrerequisiteInstaller.exe** tool to detect and install any pre-requisites.

Following the pre-requisite installation, run the **Setup.exe** tool. Accept the default suggested options; ensure for the **Server Type** you select **Stand-alone**, which is a simplified set up for development and trial environments only. With this installation all of the components will be installed on a single server as well as SQL Server Express will be installed.

As per the Microsoft recommendation, the installation wizard will ask for a SQL Server admin account and password. This account will become the Farm Account and SharePoint 2013 services will run under that identity. This account must be different from the account that you will use for your development. The SQL Server account can be a local account if the database is installed locally. It must be a domain account if the database runs on other computers. SharePoint 2013 will not allow your apps to install if the SQL Server admin account and the account that you use for installing apps for SharePoint are the same.

After your SharePoint 2013 installation is complete, you will be prompted to start the **SharePoint Products and Technologies Configuration Wizard**.

Once the configuration wizard has completed the set up, create a default site with a chosen template. We'll learn all about templates further in the book, for the purposes of completing the installation choose the **Team Site** template from the list.

For the overview part of this book, you will not need development tools; however, for the remaining scenarios you will need Visual Studio 2012 installed in your development machine. Search TechNet for *Installing Visual Studio 2012* for detailed steps on installing the Visual Studio 2012.

Your environment set up

1.2 SharePoint Central Administration

SharePoint 2013 Central Administration is a dedicated administrative site which you can also see in IIS manager and its primary role is to help administrators perform tasks around SharePoint 2013 administration, maintenance, and server-wide configuration from a central location.

You can access the Central Administration site from IIS manager by opening the web site named: **SharePoint Central Administration** or by opening a link from your start menu.

Since this book is not an administration guide, we'll only be touching Central Administration a few times, mainly for application management where we need to add or delete SharePoint sites, and verify configuration of services.

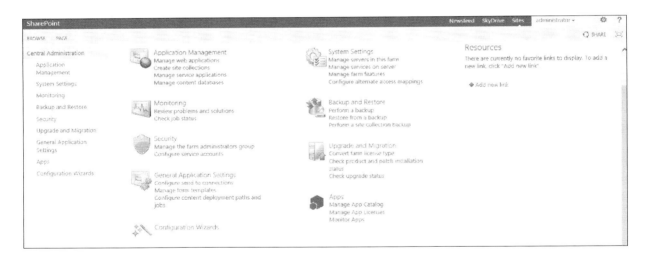

Figure 1.2.1 Central Administration home page

CHAPTER 2

Overview of major collaboration components in SharePoint 2013

In this chapter:

- Overview of site templates
- Publishing Portal
- Team Site
- Community Site
- Project Site
- Enterprise WIKI
- Enterprise Search Center
- Personal Site
- How does it all fit together

2.1 Overview of site templates

Site templates in SharePoint are a logical construct so they're not tied to hardware or network components; it's an important piece because it ties a set of functionality to a business function. The set of functionality it ties together can be: pages, controls, web parts, apps, event handlers, event receivers and other custom or out-of-the-box components.

Administrators and power users can create instances of out-of-the-box and custom site templates and those instances become sites or site collections. Essentially this operation will create several records in a database defining new site or site collection instance and its related functionality, permissions, etc.

Sites and site collections will inherit all the functions defined in the template and you can customize them and add new features which weren't originally in the template to make new templates that fit your needs. You can also save this new customized site instance into a new template and use it as a starting point to build sites from.

We'll take a look at several out-of-the-box site templates below with the focus on collaboration features and how you can use them. Further in the book, we'll take a look at how you can customize those templates with Visual Studio.

The more simple and close to out-of-the-box functionality you keep your templates, the easier it is to transfer and use those on other environments, and the simpler it is tvo upgrade them in the future to a new version of SharePoint.

2.2 Publishing Portal

What is it

Publishing Portal in its primary function contains a set of features aimed at facilitating web content management. Since we're building a collaboration solution, you might think: "What does web content management have to do with my collaboration solution?" You're correct, web content management is not our primary goal. However, as you'll see in the usage scenarios below, many collaboration solutions are wrapped in a thin layer of web content, so having web content management functionality provides the necessary flexibility to build better collaboration solutions.

The web content management features mentioned above include:

- Simplified site navigation management and ability to drive navigation based on taxonomy instead of site structure
- Design Manager which simplifies site branding and user interface customizations
- Snippet Gallery containing additional publishing features and web parts to facilitate querying and rendering of content
- Device Channeling allowing you to customize rendering of your content depending on the type of device the end-user is using
- Automatic image rendition creation to help tailor graphics to a type of content
- Cross-site content publishing allowing you to reuse content across multiple sites

The above features add useful functionality to any collaboration solution. In fact, many collaboration solutions such as intranets, extranets, partner sites, and board sites, make use of the above features to help the end-users navigate through the collaboration site and help content-authors with defining one source of the truth.

Overview of major collaboration components in SharePoint 2013

Where it belongs

Typically the publishing site template is used as your parent site template when users log into the site. The idea here is to avoid throwing users right into a bunch of documents and calendars as soon as they log in but give them a "home" area where they land and choose where to go to. Many organizations also choose to entertain their end-users on this home area providing content such as: tips, KPI's, latest news, weather, etc. It's important not to get carried away with all the fluff and keep the home area entertainingly useful. It's also recommended to keep this area light so that users can get to where they need quickly without taking a hike through a forest of navigation menus.

How to create it

Since a Publishing Site is typically the home or a landing area for other sites, it will reside in the root site collection of your web application.

To create a new root site collection of a Publishing Site template follows these steps:

1. Navigate to the **Central Administration** site
2. On the left hand side navigation menu, click **Application Management**
3. To ensure you don't have any existing site collections at the desired URL, click **Delete a site collection** link
4. From the **Site Collection** drop down, select **Change Site Collection** option
5. From the dialog window ensure the selected site collection is the root site collection with the URL '/' as shown below.
6. Click **OK**

Figure 2.2.1 Site collection picker

7. Click the **Delete** button and confirm the deletion
8. Now click the **Create site collections** link
9. Provide the site collection information as follows:
    a. Title: Home
    b. URL: '/'
    c. Select a template: **Publishing | Publishing Portal**
    d. Primary Site Collection Administrator: [administrator]
10. Leave the rest of the settings as set by default and click **OK**
11. Ensure the site has created after and you can access it when clicking on the provided link

How to manage its content

Once you have created the Publishing Site instance you will get a default landing pages provisioned.

To edit an existing page in place, click the **Gear Menu** while on the page you want to edit and select **Edit Page**, as shown below:

Overview of major collaboration components in SharePoint 2013

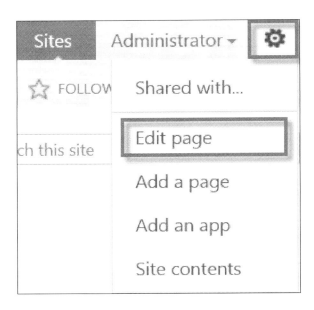

Figure 2.2.2 Editing page content

Once in **Edit** mode, you will be able to make changes to the page such as editing its content and add web parts to designated zones, marked with an **Add a Web Part** buttons. As you scroll the default page, you will see that web part zones have been placed in a particular order and have specific width. We will see how you can define your own zones or change how much space existing zones take in a scenario titled *Provisioning and applying your own custom page layouts* later in this book. To change a page layout and the subsequent zones available on it, click the **Page** tab on the ribbon and find the **Page Actions** group, from there select the **Page Layout** fly out menu. Here you can pick any of the out-of-the-box page layouts and see how page zones change with them.

The ribbon on the top of the page will display relevant controls depending on the section you're working with; which is similar in its behavior with MS Office applications.

When you scroll the page down and click the **Add a Web Part** button on one of the zones, you will have the ability to select a web part from a category and add it to the page. We will take a look at the functionality of some web parts and apps in the following section.

When done editing the page, you have an option to **Save** the page in the **Page** ribbon tab; another option is **Save and Publish**. When the page is published it's available for others to view so use the Publish option when you're ready to show your changes to others.

To add a new page to the site, click the **Gear Menu** and select **Add a Page**. When the new page is created you will have access to the same editing features described above.

All pages you have created on the site will reside in the **Pages** library. You can access the library and view the pages: click the **Gear Menu | Site Contents |** click the link to the **Pages** library.

You can access additional options of the page such as share it with others or delete it by clicking the ellipsis icon as shown below:

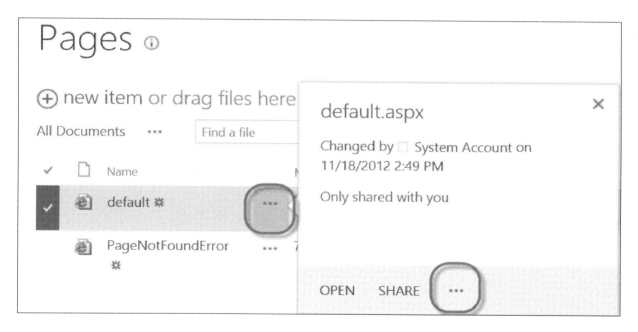

Figure 2.2.3 Accessing page properties and additional options

For more information on how to manage content automatically using automated scripts and Visual Studio solutions see the scenario entitled *Extending publishing and other site templates*.

Overview of major collaboration components in SharePoint 2013

Collaboration essentials

Now that you know how to add and remove content on the site, let's take a look at important web parts and other features which you will be using on a Publishing Site.

Content Query Web Part

The Content Query Web Part is designed to query the site for a particular type of content based on the predefined query and surface it on the page you choose. This web part is only available for sites of a Publishing Site template or sites with a Publishing Infrastructure site feature enabled, as we'll discuss further. It can be added to the page by clicking **Add a Web Part** while the page is in the edit mode. From The **Category** select **Content Rollup**. The web part will have a link to a tool pane, where you can configure it.

The Content Query Web Part returns items, which can be pages, documents, etc; that are on the current site collection. In other words, if you create another site collection just like we did with the Publishing Site, the content of this site collection can not be queried and returned by the Content Query Web Part in your Publishing Site.

The **Query** section of the web part allows you to set where your content comes from. Typically the web part is used to roll up news articles which reside in the specific area of the site collection and rolled up to the home page.

What's great about the Content Query Web Part is that it can return content from the specific list or search for all content in all lists on the site collection which inherit from a particular **content type**.

A content type is used to classify content in SharePoint similar to how file types are classified on your computer. On top of basic metadata such as date created, size, name, and more, SharePoint content types can carry an additional set of metadata which can uniquely describe a type of content. For example, a publishing page we created uses a content type called "Publishing Page". If you choose to define your own type of page, say "News Page", you can create one by inheriting all of the existing metadata from the "Publishing Page" and adding your own metadata, such as "Author Name", etc. To see how you can create a custom SharePoint content type search "creating content types in SharePoint" at http://office.microsoft.com

As suggested above, by using a Content Query Web Part you can choose to roll up a specific or custom Content Type from anywhere in the site collection. Below is a screenshot of this configuration:

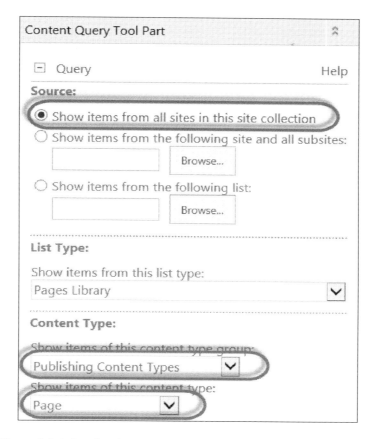

Figure 2.2.4 Configuring the query of the content query web part

If you chose to filter your results the web part will let you choose from the set of metadata fields available for this particular content type.

Among other options, the Content Query Web Part allows you to choose from a few presentation templates. The templates you can chose from can be found in the **Styles** category as shown below:

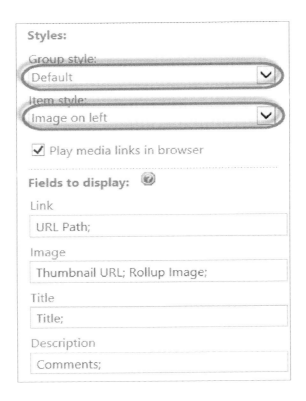

Figure 2.2.5 Configuring the presentation options of the content query web part

The styles defined rely on the fact that the content has certain metadata fields to grab information from; so if you chose to create a new content type, make sure you inherit it from a content type that already has the fields you like, that way the Content Query Web Part will have a pre-defined style for it and you won't have to make customizations.

For more information on configuring the Content Query Web Part, search for *SharePoint content query web part* at *http://office.microsoft.com.*

Content Search Web Part

The Content Search Web Part shows items that are results of a search query you define. It can be added to the page by clicking **Add a Web Part** while the page is in the edit mode. From The **Category** select **Content Search**. When added and configured, this Web Part will show recently modified items from the current site or another site. As new content is discovered by the search engine, this Web Part will display an updated list of items each time the page is viewed.

To access the Content Search Web Part configuration options, open its context menu and select Edit Web Part, as shown below:

Figure 2.2.6 Web part context menu

 The Content Search Web Part assumes that you have a running instance of the Search Service Application in your environment and that the service application has run at least one crawl. To see how to create and configure the Search Service Application, search for Create and configure a new Search service application at MSDN.

The key configuration option for the Search Query Web Part is to define a search query to return your results. In the web part editing pane, under the **Search Criteria** category, click the **Change Query** button.

You will see a **Query Builder** tool allowing you to configure the query and preview the results. The query builder is used in many other web parts to simplify query building.

In your query builder, ensure you are in the **Basics** page, in here define the following values:

- Select a query set to **Recently changed items**
- Restrict results by app set to **Don't restrict results by app**
- Restrict by tag set to **Don't restrict by any tag**

At this point you should see the Search Results Preview return results. Now switch to the **Refiners** tab of the Query Builder. In the list of refiners you will see a collection of crawled metadata on which you can refine content. The refiner metadata will appear depending on the content that's already filtered in the **Basics** tab; for example: you will not see "page" specific metadata to refine on if you selected to filter all results by "document" type of content. The rest of the Query Builder tabs are for additional settings and to view the actual search query. In our case, we will accept the configuration from the Query Builder by clicking OK.

Going back to the web part options pane, the next important section is **Display Templates**. This section allows you to choose how the results are going to be rendered. The most common options are: List, List with Paging and Slideshow. Each of the options also allows you to choose how you'd like to see the content displayed including the position of the image (if any) and the title.

Right below Display Templates category, you will see **Property Mappings** which allows you to define which fields are going to be rendered in the web part. The default values are *Title* and a link to an item. Those fields are going to be rendered according to the display template we looked at before.

The rest of the options are either less relevant to our collaboration scenario or something that you can experiment with, so click OK in the web part tool pane and view the results on the page.

The search results are very similar to those returned in Content Query Web Part but if you had content residing in multiple site collections, only the Search Query Web Part would have been able to pick up content from those other site collections.

Relevant Documents Web Part

This web part allows you to roll up documents from existing site collections which are relevant to the user who is viewing the page. The relevancy can be defined in the following way:

- Display documents that have been last **modified** by the user
- Display documents that have been **created** by the user
- Display documents that have been **checked out** by the user

When added to the page, access the web part tool pane and open the **Data** group; that's where you can configure the options above, as well as how many results you'd like to see on the page.

Other content roll up web parts

Other content roll up web parts which your users may find useful, include several web parts from the **Search-Driven Content** category. Those are:

- **Pictures** Web Part – which shows any items that are derived from the Picture or Image content type. In essence this web part is a version of a **Content Search** Web Part allowing you to build queries, refine items, and chose rendering styles.

- **Videos** Web Part – same as **Pictures** Web Part above but geared towards video content types.

- **Web Pages** Web Part – same as above but will display a list of web pages similar to the ones we created earlier in this scenario. This is one of the ways to allow your users to navigate through key pages representing the root of your site.

- **Popular Items** Web Part - is also a version of a **Content Search** Web Part allowing you to build queries, refine items, and chose rendering styles. The web part logic, however, is aimed at displaying the most popular content as determined by the built in analytics service. The analytics service in SharePoint collects usage information and feeds it into the search system to deliver better search experience and facilitate web parts which use search.

- **Recently Changed Items** Web Part- will show items that have been modified recently, helping your users to track the latest activity on a site.

Overview of major collaboration components in SharePoint 2013

Must have web parts

Among the web parts that enhance the user experience, below are few web parts that can be useful on any site. All of the below web parts can be found in the **Media and Content** web part category:

- **Content Editor** – is the most used web part to add content to your pages. When added to the page, you will be able to type in content as is and format your content with the formatting tools as shown below:

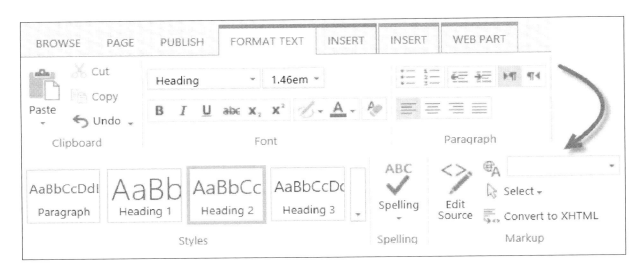

Figure 2.2.7 Ribbon options for content editor web part

- **Script Editor** – is a placeholder for JavaScript and HTML which you may want to inject on the page. Although this method of customization is more ad-hoc, it's still acceptable if only one or two pages need to be customized

2.3 Team Site

What is it

The Team Site template contains a set of features allowing end users to work together, share documents, assign tasks and track input. It also allows users to share their thoughts in a newsfeed like fashion. There are several usage scenarios for a team site, described in the sections below.

Where it belongs

A Team Site typically resides as a sub site under the root site of your site collection. There is nothing that can really stop you from making your root site a team site; however, the team site template doesn't come with a set of feature which make a good landing area for an intranet, extranet or board site. More about those features in the **Publishing Portal | What is it** section above.

A Team site can be used for a variety of sites with the main goal of allowing the team to share calendars, tasks, and project related documents. Here are few examples of sites where the team site template makes sense:

- Project site
- Workgroup site
- Department site
- Committee site

The key differentiator between other site templates is that documents and content on a team site are going to start in their draft version and evolve through the means of team collaboration to a final version. So it's a place to collaborate and track tasks related to collaboration.

How to create it

If you're going to create a team site under the Publishing root site, you first need to enable the team site template:

1. While on your Publishing root site, click the **Gear Menu** and select **Site Settings**
2. Under the **Look and Feel** click **Page layouts and site templates**
3. From the list of **Subsite templates** locate the **Team Site** and click **Add** to make it available

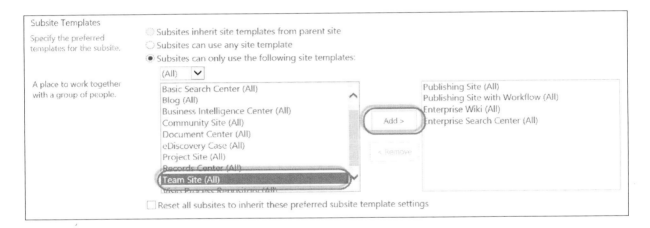

Figure 2.3.1 Adding new allowed sub site templates

4. Click **OK**.

Now, to create an instance of a team site:

1. While on your Publishing root site home page, click the **Gear Menu** and select **Site Contents**
2. Scroll to the bottom until you see the **Sub-sites** group, click **+ new subsite**
3. Specify the following values in the form provided:
   a. Title: **Sustainability**

b. URL: **Sustainability**
c. Template: **Collaboration | Team Site**
4. Leave the rest of the options as-is and click the **Create** button.

How to manage its content

To edit the landing page of the team site, click on the **Gear Menu** and select **Edit Page**. You'll be presented with an area to type your content right on the page; as well as you can change the format of the text using the contextual ribbon as shown below.

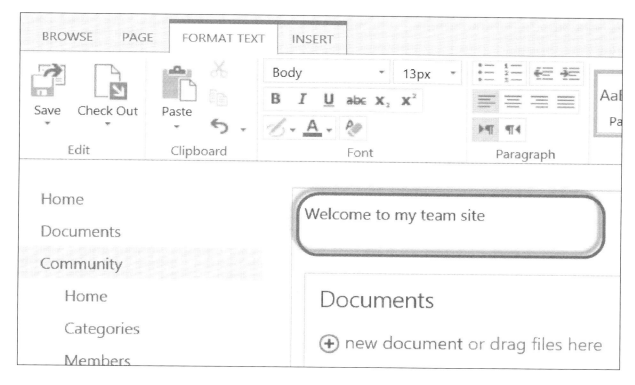

Figure 2.3.2 Editing the content of the team site page

Additionally, you can insert a web part on the page by using the **Insert | Web part** options from the ribbon. When ready, you can save your changes on the page by clicking the **Page** tab from the ribbon followed by the **Save** ribbon button.

Overview of major collaboration components in SharePoint 2013

To create a new page, click the **Gear Menu**, and select **Add a Page**. When requested provide the page name and note the URL the page will have, and click **Create**.
You will see a newly created blank page which you can edit just like the existing home page; when ready click **Save**.

All of the pages will be created under the **Site Pages** library, which you can access by clicking the **Gear Menu | Site Contents | Site Pages**.

If the page you have created is significant enough to be in one of the navigation menus, you can add it to the site by using the steps outlined in the **Important features and configurations | Team site navigation** section below.

Collaboration essentials

Calendar App

The SharePoint calendar is a popular feature allowing your team members to share group events and share a schedule. To add a calendar app:

1. Click the **Gear Menu** and select **Add an app**
2. From the list below under **Apps you can add** click **Calendar**
3. In the popup to follow set the **Name** to **Calendar**

You will be taken to a **Site Contents** page where you can select our newly created calendar app. You can add new events and navigate through month and day views. You'll notice that when you hover over a day to add a new event, the form you will see will collect a predefined set of metadata such as **Title**, **Description**, etc. You can actually customize what metadata is collected and add new pieces of metadata to be collected each time a user creates or edits a calendar event. To do that:

1. Return to the calendar view and in the ribbon of the page, click on the **Calendar** tab
2. In the **Settings** group of the ribbon click the **List Settings** button
3. Scroll down to the **Columns** group where you will see all of the available metadata columns defined for the list

Chapter 2

Columns		
\multicolumn{3}{l}{A column stores information about each item in the list. Because this list allows m}

Columns

A column stores information about each item in the list. Because this list allows m whether information is required or optional for a column, are now specified by th currently available in this list:

Column (click to edit)	Type	Used in
Attendees	Person or Group	
Category	Choice	Event
Check Double Booking	Check Double Booking	
Created	Date and Time	
Description	Multiple lines of text	Event
End Time	Date and Time	Event
Free/Busy	Free/Busy	
Location	Single line of text	Event
Modified	Date and Time	

Figure 2.3.3 Calendar metadata fields

4. Click the **Category** column and scroll through the available options. This type of column is a **Choice** column allowing administrators to choose options available to users to pick from and how they're presented. Scroll down to the bottom and click the **Delete** button and confirm the deletion

5. On the next page, which is the **List Settings** page, add a new column by clicking the **Create column** link in the **Columns** group

6. Specify the following values for the new column:

    a. Column name: **Confirmation Required**
    b. The type of information in this column is: **Yes/No (check box)**
    c. Click **OK**

With above steps we have deleted an existing column called **Category** and added a new column called **Confirmation Required**. When you return back to the Calendar app and add a new event, you will see that the **Category** is no longer collected and our new check box

Overview of major collaboration components in SharePoint 2013

column is there instead.
You can also add the calendar app to the home page of your team site by editing the home page and selecting ribbon tab **Page** | **Insert** | **App part**. From the list of app parts you will see the **Calendar**.

Team site navigation

A Team site has top navigation and quick launch navigation, both of which you can edit. To edit your quick launch or top navigation, click the **Edit Links** button beside the corresponding navigation as shown below and adjust which items you would like to remove and any new items you may want to add:

Figure 2.3.4 Managing site navigation

Announcements app

Announcements is another app which can be used to broadcast announcements. It can be added in a similar fashion to the Calendar app by clicking the **Gear Menu | Add an app |** and select the **Announcements** app. When requested, provide the name for the app: **Announcements**.

Similar to a calendar you can add an announcement and modify its required metadata just like the **Calendar** app above.

Other important apps

Among other apps which follow the behavior of Calendar and Announcements in their usage and configuration are the following apps:

1. **Links** app – allows users to enter and share links. This is typically used on the home page of a team site to share useful external or internal links to members of the team site
2. **Tasks** app – this app allows users to assign and track tasks manually or by automated processes described later in this section
3. **Contacts** app – helps users to enter and share contact information with other site members. Since this app collects many metadata fields which you may not need – you can use the same principle as described in the Calendar app to remove or add your own metadata fields
4. **Issue tracking** app – allows users to enter and track metadata related to an issue
5. **Survey** app – allows users to build and collect survey responses

Documents library

The Documents library exists on newly created team sites but you can add new instances of it to store any specific information you want to keep separate from the Documents library created by default.

The library can store metadata related information and carry it over with the actual content. You can choose additional metadata for each document just like in the example with the **Calendar**.

Overview of major collaboration components in SharePoint 2013

When you add new content to the library, you can perform actions on it, including sharing it with others, editing its metadata, downloading a copy, triggering workflows on the content, etc.

Figure 2.3.5 Additional options available for document library content

Approval and Feedback workflows

SharePoint has several workflows available for content on a site; most common are Approval and Feedback, which are two distinct workflows. The Approval workflow allows a content author to launch an approval on a piece of content; an approval may start automatically when a piece of content is added to a library. An approval can have predefined approvers or approvers can be picked at the time of the workflow initiation.

In order to be available to be triggered, an approval or feedback workflow must be associated with the library. Here is how to associate an approval workflow to a **Documents** library available on a team site by default:

1. Click the **Documents** link from the quick launch navigation on your team site
2. From the ribbon select the **Library** tab | in the **Settings** group | click **Workflow Settings** | click **Add a workflow** as shown below

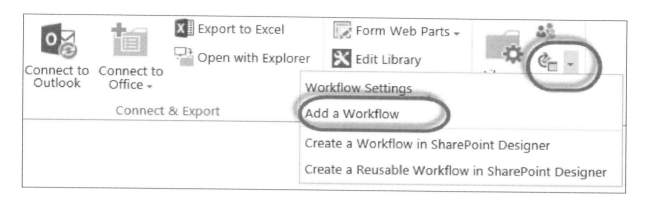

Figure 2.3.6 Workflow settings for lists and libraries

3. Set the following values on the association page:
    a. Select a workflow template: **Approval – SharePoint 2010**
    b. Type a unique name for this workflow: **Approval**
    c. Leave the rest of the options as-is. Take a note of the **Start Options** to see how to set workflow to initiate automatically on the newly created items.
4. Click **Next**

Additional configuration options are available on a next page specific to our Approval workflow. Those will drive the execution process of a workflow.

2.4 Community Site

What is it

Community Site is a template designed to engage users in a moderated exchange of ideas, promote discussions, and reward members who are the most active in the community.

Where it belongs

A Community Site typically resides as a sub site under the root site of your site collection. Depending on the usage scenario you can also have a community site residing under the overarching space for communities in a larger intranet scenario. As you'll see below, it's also appropriate to create a community site under the team site representing a landing page for the community.

A Community site is most commonly used in the following scenarios:

- Crowdsourcing site
- Workgroup idea site
- Committee idea site

As you can see, some of the usage scenarios above overlap with the ones we looked when discussing a **Team Site**. For example, the **Workgroup** site scenario. However, in the case of a workgroup site using a community site template, ultimately it is meant to engage members to brainstorm ideas and draft decisions. Where as the workgroup site using a team site template, is more focused on providing a final product of such ideas in the form of documents and deliverables; those can still be in a draft form but beyond the initial crowdsourcing phase. Therefore the community site, as you'll see in the **Collaboration essentials** section below, contains more tools and features facilitating frequent and non-structured interaction between members. For larger communities, you will also find tools helping moderators to recognize the most active contributors.

How to create it

In our case, we will create a community site under the team site called **Sustainability** discussed earlier in this scenario. The parent team site will be accessible to all users, where the community site will only be used by the members of the Sustainability working group.

To create an instance of a community site under the existing team site:

1. While on the Sustainability team site home page , click the **Gear Menu** and select **Site Settings**
2. Click **Site Collection Features** | locate the feature titled **SharePoint Server Standard Site Collection features** | ensure the feature is marked as **Active**.
3. Click the **Gear Menu** and select **Site Contents**
4. Scroll to the bottom until you see the **Sub-sites** group, click **+ new subsite**
5. Specify the following values in the form provided:
    a. Title: **Sustainability brainstorming**
    b. URL: **SustainabilityBrainstorming**
    c. Template: **Collaboration | Community Site**
    d. User Permissions: **Use unique permissions**

Leave the rest of the options as-is and click the **Create** button. On the following page you will be prompted to create new security groups for our site with unique permissions. Accept all the defaults and proceed to create security groups as suggested by SharePoint.

How to manage its content

To edit the landing page of the community site, click on the **Gear Menu** and select **Edit Page**. You will be presented with an area to type your content right on the page; as well as you can change the format of the text using the contextual ribbon options.

There are other pages on the community site which display various web parts for the community members, content on those can be edited in a similar fashion as above. Those pages can be found by clicking the **Gear Menu** | **Site Contents** | **Site Pages** library.

Overview of major collaboration components in SharePoint 2013

The main type of content on the community site are discussions; to create new discussion you can either use a **+new discussion** link on the home page or navigating to the discussions list: **Gear Menu | Site Contents | Discussion List**.

To add new discussion, users can use either **+new discussion** link or ribbon button in the discussion list. Basic metadata about the discussion topic is collected when the item is created, this includes: Subject, Body, Question, and Category. You can add or remove the required metadata just as discussed earlier in this scenario.

To keep discussion items relevant to a particular category, the community site uses a categories list. You can edit and add categories by navigating to the category list: **Gear Menu | Site Contents | Categories** list.

To add a new category item, click the **Items** ribbon tab and select **New Item** button. In here you can provide a name and description for the category as well as a picture.

The main types of content on the community site are discussions, and there are few tools to manage those which we'll discuss next.

Collaboration essentials

Unique permissions

When we created the community site earlier, we chose the option to use unique permissions for our site. This means those users who have access to the parent site may not necessarily have access to the community site. This configuration allows only the community members who have access to the community site to see it rolled up in the navigation, and have access to it.

The concept of unique permissions isn't unique to a community site and you can have unique permissions on any of the sites. In fact, you can have unique permissions on document libraries, lists and documents. Be careful, however, when giving away unique permissions to documents or items on a site, it becomes difficult to manage highly customized permissions. What happens is that when you add a new member to a site which has been around for a while, you may assume they have access to everything on that site, however, if you have customized permissions on the site – that user may constantly be missing access to some items.

By default, when a new site is created with unique permissions, SharePoint creates a few default security groups to which you can add members. To see those groups, click the **Gear Menu** | select **Site Settings** | click on the **Site Permissions** link.

Here is how the permissions management screen will look like for our **Sustainability Brainstorming** site:

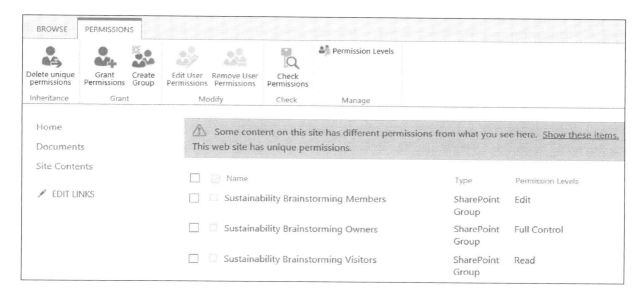

Figure 2.4.1 Managing site permissions

To add user to a group, let's say a **Moderator** group, click on the **Sustainability Brainstorming Moderators** link | click the **New** button | type in user Id of a new user | click **Share**.

Now your user has been given access to the functionality which is only given to members of the moderator group.

 You can always reset the site to inherit the permissions from its parent and remove any expectations and users which might have been given permissions directly. Keep in mind that if someone had a special access to the site and not its parent, as soon as you set the site to inherit permissions from the parent, those special users will lose access to all such exception items. To configure your site with permission inheritance, click the Gear Menu | select Site Settings | click on the Site Permissions link | click Delete unique permissions button on the ribbon | click OK on the prompts.

Overview of major collaboration components in SharePoint 2013

Managing discussions

If you are a member of the community site owners security group, you will have access to manage discussions on the site. You can access the discussion management tools from the community site home page | **Community tools** and clicking on the **Manage discussions**. Alternatively, you can navigate to the discussions list view: click **Site Gear Menu** | select **Site Contents** | click the **Discussions List** | in the ribbon select the **List** tab | from the **Current View** dropdown select **Management**.

By clicking on the ellipsis icon for the selected discussion item, you can view or edit details of the discussion as well as delete the item. In essence, the discussion item is as any other SharePoint list item and you can even run workflows on it if required.

You can also mark or unmark the discussion as **Featured**, which will make it appear in the **Featured** list on the home page. To do that, select the discussion item while in the **Discussion** list and in the **Moderation** ribbon tab, select either **Mark** or **Unmark as Featured**.

User can also report the particular post to a moderator to ensure quality content on the site:

Chapter 2

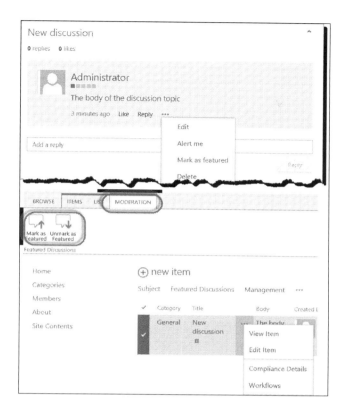

Figure 2.4.2 Discussion management tools

You can review such reported content by clicking the **View reported posts** link on the home page. The link will essentially take you to the **Discussion List** filtered by a metadata field which marks the post as reported. Several users can report the same post and the moderator can see the number of reports to help them make a decision.

From the reported view, the moderator can view details of the report and dismiss the report if applicable or they can edit or delete the post, see the options from the **Moderation** tab in the ribbon as shown in the screenshot above.

 If you're unable to see the option to report discussions, you may need to enable the feature. You can enable the report to moderator feature in Community tools web part and by clicking the Community settings link. That page can also be accessed from the Gear Menu | Site Settings | Community Settings. Once on the settings page, ensure the Enable reporting of offensive content check box is on and click OK.

— 41 —

Member reputation management

To ensure quality input into the community is recognized, the community site has several tools available for moderators and administrators to measure community engagement.

To review those settings, in the **Community tools** web part on the home page, click the **Reputation settings** link. Alternatively, you can access the same page by clicking the **Gear Menu | Site Settings |** find the **Community Administration** category | and select **Reputation Settings**.

In here you will be able to select whether posts can be rated or not and whether they are rated by Like or a 5 Star system.

You can also define various member achievements for your users based on the number of points they receive, and also define how many points they receive for each of the following activities:

- Creating a new post
- Replying to a post
- Member's post or reply gets liked or receives a rating of 4 or 5 stars
- Member's reply gets marked as 'Best Reply'

Upon achieving a certain level, users can receive a text or a graphic badge.

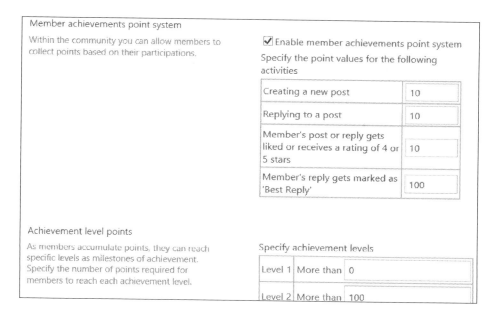

Figure 2.4.3 Managing achievements and points

You can also manage a list of badges and gift badges to your members for special achievements.

The list of badges can be accessed from the **Reputation Settings** page by clicking the **Manage the list of gifted badges** link. The badge is just a name entered into a list.

To gift a badge to a member:

1. Navigate to the Members list (**Members** link on the quick launch)
2. In the **Community tools** web part, click on **Assign badges to members** | select a member
3. Click the **Moderation** ribbon tab
4. Click the **Give Badge** ribbon button
5. Select the badge from the list
6. Click **Save**

A member can only have one badge so if they had a previous badge, it would be overwritten.

2.5 Project Site

What is it

A Project site instance is essentially a collaboration area for a project where users can create tasks, share documents and track calendar events.

Where it belongs

The Project site template is composed from essentially the same components as a team site, apart from a few small differences outlined below. A Project site usually resides under the overarching landing area for all projects. In our case, we could have a "Projects" team site under the root site which will serve as the landing area for all the other projects living under our "Projects" landing site.

In other scenarios, projects can spin off of the community ideas or workgroups, in which case it's appropriate to have a project site as a sub site of a community site or a workgroup site.

Just as any other SharePoint site, you can assign unique permissions to a project site so only members of a particular project have the appropriate level of access to their site.

How to create it

In our case, we will create a Projects landing area site under our root site. The parent projects landing site will be accessible to all users, while individual project sites could be set up with more restrictive access, in our case users will have the same level of access to both the projects landing site as well as our individual projects.

To create an instance of a project landing site under our root site:

1. While on the root site home page , click the **Gear Menu** and select **Site Contents**
2. Scroll to the bottom until you see the **Sub-sites** group, click **+ new subsite**
3. Specify the following values in the form provided:

a. Title: **Projects**
   b. URL: **Projects**
   c. Template: **Collaboration | Team Site**

Leave the rest of the options as-is and click the **Create** button

Next, to create an instance of a specific project site under our projects landing site:

1. While on the projects landing site, click the **Gear Menu** and select **Site Contents**
2. Scroll to the bottom until you see the **Sub-sites** group, click **+ new subsite**
3. Specify the following values in the form provided:

   a. Title: **Platform Upgrade Project**
   b. URL: **PlatformUpgrade**
   c. Template: **Collaboration | Project Site**

Leave the rest of the options as-is and click the **Create** button

How to manage its content

As mentioned above, a project site is essentially a team site with couple of differences. This means that the page editing experience is exactly the same as we've already seen on the team site.

One item you will notice is that our project site has a Project Summary timeline. This feature connects to the out-of-the-box instance of a SharePoint task list and rolls up all tasks created in the list into this view.

To add a new task you simply click the **Edit** button in the *Get organized. Edit the task list* area. Alternatively, you can access the same interface by clicking **Site Contents** on the quick launch and clicking the **Tasks** list. From here you can manage existing tasks or create new tasks.

From the home page you can edit the Project Summary web part by switching to the edit mode of the page, click on the **Gear Menu** and select **Edit Page**. Access the context menu of the Project Summary web part and select **Edit Web Part**.

Overview of major collaboration components in SharePoint 2013

From here you will be able to select another task list, if you have several of them, as well as choose whether to display late or upcoming tasks.

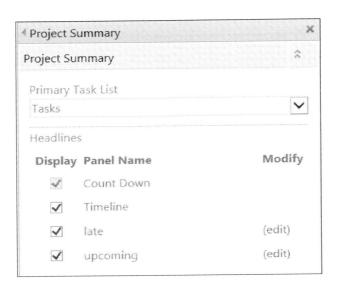

Figure 2.5.1 Project summary web part properties

All the other settings of this web part are out-of-the-box configurations available in all the other SharePoint web parts.

By clicking the timeline on the Project Summary web part, you will see the ribbon tab called **Timeline**; from here you will be able to choose additional fields you can hide or display, as well as several formatting preferences:

Figure 2.5.2 Timeline settings

Chapter 2

Just as with any other SharePoint web part, you can have two or more instances of the web part on the page each connected to its own **Task** list and display various tasks. You can define several task lists, for example: Issues and Milestones; those can be then rendered in their respective project summary web parts.

Collaboration essentials

Tasks and Sub tasks

As we have seen above, to create a new task on a project site you would access the **Task** list on the site or click **Edit** in the **Project Summary** web part on the home page of the site. When creating a new task, your task may have nothing but the title. However, to make the task show up in the timeline or Project Summary web part, you also need to enter start and end dates.

By accessing the context menu of the task, you can create a sub task; each sub task may have its own sub tasks allowing you to track dependencies. When you delete a parent task, all child tasks are deleted.

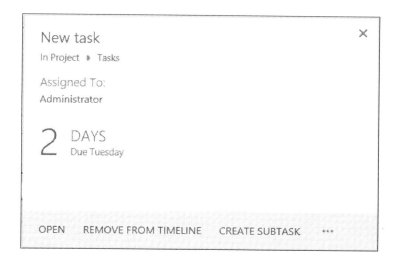

Figure 2.5.3 Managing tasks and related items

Overview of major collaboration components in SharePoint 2013

You can run workflows on a task the same way you can run workflows on other SharePoint list items, for example calendar events. You can also edit the task list to collect additional metadata or delete existing metadata columns.

Out-of-the-box metadata values collected by the task include:

- Task Name
- Start Date
- Due Date
- Assigned To
- % Complete
- Description
- Predecessors
- Priority
- Task Status
- Related Items
- Completed
- Created
- Modified

2.6 Enterprise WIKI

What is it

The Enterprise WIKI Site is a site template designed to enable users to capture semi structured data (How to articles, procedures, manuals, etc.) and share it with others. The wiki infrastructure allows other users to give feedback on the quality of the content and rank it.

Where it belongs

Depending on the role of a WIKI site, it may be best suited as a child of a root site. In our example, we'll create a site for **Policies and Procedures** which will reside right off the root site.

Here are few other ways for which you can use an Enterprise WIKI site:

- Glossary site
- "How To" library
- Policies and Procedures site
- Manuals library
- Corporate Processes

As you may have noticed the overarching trend here is that above usage scenarios call for a container which can store articles which can be categorized. Those articles are easily searchable and you can preview them very quickly because those are just pages and you don't need to open documents. This means if you have a usage scenario calling for the same set of capabilities you're free to use the Enterprise WIKI for that scenario.

I have seen the Enterprise WIKI being used to create a software solution design. Something you would probably use a Word document for, but purely because it was so easy to create and co-author WIKI pages and see the hierarchy being built as the design evolved – it was a really good choice. In this case the WIKI site was created under an individual project site.

How to create it

In our case, we will create an Enterprise WIKI site under the root site. The site will be accessible to all users.

Assuming our root site is a **Publishing Site** we have all the necessary pre-requisites to create an Enterprise WIKI under it. However, if the parent for your WIKI site is not a Publishing Site, you will need to enable Publishing Features to have the option to create a child WIKI site. To enable this, follow the steps below:

1. Navigate to the site under which you would like to create an Enterprise WIKI site.
2. Click the **Gear Menu** and select **Site Settings**
3. Scroll to **Site Collection Administration** and click on **Site collection features**
4. Locate the feature titled **SharePoint Server Publishing Infrastructure** and click **Activate** right beside it
5. Ensure you have received a response indicating that the feature has been activated

To create an instance of an Enterprise WIKI site under the existing root site:

1. Click the **Gear Menu** and select **Site Contents**
2. Scroll to the bottom until you see the **Sub-sites** group, click **+ new subsite**
3. Specify the following values in the form provided:
    a. Title: **Policies and Procedures**
    b. URL: **PoliciesAndProcedures**
    c. Template: **Publishing | Enterprise WIKI**

Leave the rest of the options as-is and click the **Create** button

How to manage its content

Enterprise WIKI sites are very similar in structure to a team site: their Home Page is a WIKI page, they have a **Pages** library where all the WIKI articles are stored; they have a document library and a picture library.

To edit the landing page of the WIKI site, click on the **Page** tab in the ribbon and select **Edit**. You will see the same page in edit mode. By default you can change the file name of the page and its content. As you start editing the content, the ribbon will light up offering you the option to select font formatting options. You will also have a few options to insert new web parts and images into the WIKI page, the functionality here is exactly as you have already seen on a team site.

One of the reasons why WIKI sites are so popular for holding semi-structured content is because you can start creating content and easily link to other content as you author it.

For example, considering you are in the edit mode of our Home Page, anywhere in the text type *[[How to print in color]]*. When you save the page, you will see that our *How to print in color* is now appearing as a link and when you click on it, SharePoint will offer you to create a new page where you can describe the steps to print things in color. Using this technique you can build a hierarchy of future content which doesn't exist yet but you're making users aware that it's coming at some point.

If you'd like to create a new page and not link it to anything you can do so by navigating to the Pages library. While on the WIKI site, click the **Gear Menu** and select **Site Contents**, select the **Pages** library. In here, in the ribbon click the **File** tab and select **New Document**. Once you add the name and the title and choose to create the page, you can find it in the library and start editing it. You can always find and link to this page by using the "[[…]]" WIKI syntax.

To insert pictures and web parts into your WIKI articles, use the **Insert** tab in the ribbon. When inserting pictures, ensure they are uploaded in the **Images** library available on the WIKI site by default.

Collaboration essentials

Configuring WIKI categories

One of the things you'll notice when editing a WIKI page is that its default page layout will offer you the option to enter a category for the WIKI page. Let's take a look at how you can configure the set of categories users can pick from.

First, categories in a WIKI page are managed by a **Managed Metadata Service Application**

Overview of major collaboration components in SharePoint 2013

which supports metadata management functionality for a variety of functions in SharePoint, and WIKI categories are a part of it. This means that you'll need to make sure the **Managed Metadata Service Application** is configured in your site. Below we'll take a look at how to make a very basic configuration for your development environment. For a production environment configuration you should consider referring to Microsoft guides (search TechNet with *managed metadata service applications in SharePoint Server 2013*).

1. From the home page of your Central Administration site, click **Manage service applications** from the **Application Management** group
2. In the ribbon, from the **Service Applications** tab, select **New**, and pick **Managed Metadata Service** from the fly out menu
3. In the modal dialog provided, enter the following values:
   a. Name: **Managed Metadata Service**
   b. Database Name: **ManagedMetadata**
   c. Application Pool: **Use existing application pool** (select one of the available)
4. Leave all the other options are offered by default and click **OK**
5. Confirm that after few seconds the dialog disappears and the new instance of the **Managed Metadata Service** is listed in the list of service applications

Now that the managed metadata service application is created, we can create a new metadata term set which can be used for our WIKI pages

1. While in the service applications page from the previous sequence, click on the **Managed Metadata Service** link you have just created
2. On the left, from the **Taxonomy Term Store** list click on the **Managed Metadata Service** root element and select **New group**
3. Give the new group a name **Portal Config**
4. Access the context menu of the newly created group and select **New Term Set**
5. Give the new term set a name **WIKI Categories**
6. Access the context menu of the newly create term set and select **Create Term**
7. Give the new term a name **Corporate**

The hierarchy will look similar to below screenshot:

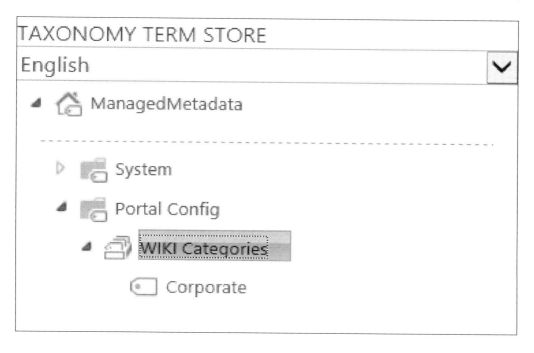

Figure 2.6.1 Taxonomy terms store

Now it's time to set this term set to be used as the WIKI categories on our WIKI site.

1. Navigate to your WIKI site and click **Site Contents** on the quick launch
2. Click the **Pages** library
3. From the ribbon, click the **Library** tab, and then click on **Library Settings** button
4. Scroll down to the section called **Content Types** and click on the link called **Enterprise WIKI Page**
5. You will see the list of all the metadata that's assigned to each instance of a WIKI page, click on the item right below called **WIKI Categories**
6. Click the **Edit column** link right beside **WIKI Categories** name
7. Scroll down to the **Term Set Settings** group and locate the **WIKI Categories** in the hierarchy of term store; ensure our term set is selected
8. Click OK on the page

Now, our end users can pick a category when creating or editing a WIKI page:

Overview of major collaboration components in SharePoint 2013

1. Navigate back to the WIKI page and edit the page
2. Click the metadata lookup button **[...]** to see a list of available terms listed from the **WIKI Categories** term set
3. Pick the **Corporate** category we created | click the **Select** button | save the page
4. The category will now appear as a link and any WIKI page that's tagged with this category can be rolled by when users click on the category link

Note that if you require a hierarchical term set, you can create a hierarchy in the managed metadata store in Central Administration.

2.7 Enterprise Search Center

What is it

The Enterprise Search Center is a special type of a site template, since you don't really store content on the search center, but use it to let your end users search the site contents. Since it a site template, all the rules of editing pages on the site still apply with the addition of some web parts and other components related to search.

Where it belongs

The Enterprise Search Center typically resides in a separate site collection with a dedicated managed path. What this means is that to most users it will look like a sub site of the root site. In the next section, we'll take a look at how to configure the search center to have its own managed path and how it's connected to the rest of the site so that when searches are triggered through a search box on the site, users are redirected to your search center.

How to create it

First, let's configure a new managed (aka virtual) path for the search center so it responds under *http://servername/search*; which is done purely so users can easily remember how to get to it if they need to.

1. From the home page of the SharePoint Central Administration click **Manage web applications** under the **Application Management** group
2. Select the web application which currently hosts your root site (ex.: SharePoint - 80)
3. From the ribbon's **Web Applications** tab, which should be selected by default, click **Managed Paths**
4. In the modal dialog which appears, set the following values, as also shown in the screenshot below:
    a. Path: **search**
    b. Type: **Explicit inclusion**

Overview of major collaboration components in SharePoint 2013

5. Click the **Add path** button and confirm that the path has been added as shown in the screenshot below
6. Click **OK**

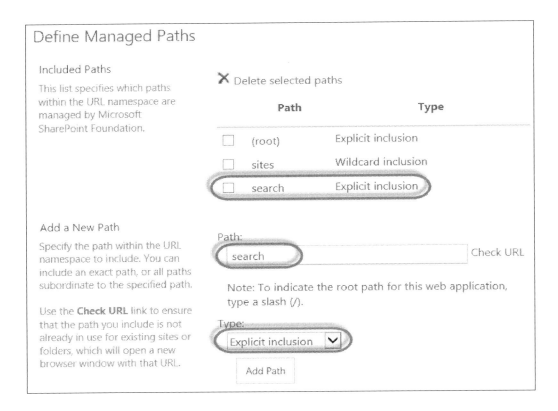

Figure 2.7.1 Defining managed paths for the search site

Now let's create the actual search center site, also from within Central Administration.

1. From the SharePoint Central Administration home page, click **Create site collections** from the **Application Management** group
2. In the page provided enter the following values
    a. Title: **Search**
    b. Url: select **/search** from the options provided
    c. Select a template: **Enterprise | Enterprise Search Center**

      d. Primary Site Collection Administrator: **[administrator username]**
3. Leave the rest of the values as set by default and click **OK**

How to manage its content

The search site is not something you'll be changing on a regular basis; however, it's important to some of the existing components here, and how you can adjust them to improve the search experience for your end users.

The first configuration you will need to complete is to connect the search box of the main site to your search center, let's take a look at how to do that:

1. Navigate to the root of your SharePoint site
2. Click the **Gear Menu** and select **Site Settings**
3. From **Site Collection Administration** group, select **Search Settings**
4. Enter the following values for the configuration parameters on the page:
       a. Search Center Url: **/search**
       b. Use the same results page settings as my parent: **uncheck**
       c. Send queries to a custom results page URL: **select**
       d. Results page URL: **/search/Pages/results.aspx**
5. Click **OK** and navigate to the root of your site
6. Try searching with any keyword in a textbox provided on the root site and ensure you are redirected to our newly created search center with the Url: *http://servername/search*

Another configuration you may see useful for your search site is adding custom or out-of-the-box web parts to make announcements to users visiting the search page, or to solicit feedback on their search experience. The out-of-the-box search center has several pages where your users might end up, you can see them all by navigating to the root of your search center and clicking the **Gear Menu**, then select **Site Contents**. Click the **Pages** library to see the following search pages:

1. **Default.aspx** – the home page of the search center, if the end user has landed on it directly. By default it contains the search box where users enter their query

2. **Advanced.aspx** – the advanced search page allowing users to refine their search by various metadata and result types. In essence this refinement will produce a more complex and precise query
3. **Results.aspx** – the main search results page returning all types of results. This page consists of the:
    a. **Search Box** web part – allowing users to define a new query
    b. **Search Navigation** web part – allowing users to refine results by: videos, conversations, reports, people, or all of the above
    c. **Search Results** web part – which display results and allows users to page through them
    d. **Refiner** web part – allowing users to refine the search results by metadata shared across relevant sets of results such as: modified date, author, etc.
4. **VideoResults.aspx** – is the same results page but filtering the result set with only video types
5. **ConversationResults.aspx** - same idea as with video results but only conversations are returned
6. **ReportsAndDataResults.aspx** – again, same as above but only reports are returned
7. **Peopleresults.aspx** -finally, same as above but only people results are returned

You can link to any of the above pages directly from any place on your site of you want to give your users the ability to search for a particular type of result. You can also customize any of the above pages with out-of-the-box or custom web parts. To edit any of the search pages, click the **Gear Menu** and select **Edit Page**.

2.8 Personal Site

What is it

A Personal site allows end users to share information about themselves with the rest of the organization, track activities in their newsfeed, track their tasks, follow documents and sites, as well as store and share personal documents.

Where it belongs

A Personal site has a very special place in a SharePoint site; you can't have a personal site under the project site or elsewhere, it has its dedicated place. A Personal site consists of two parts:

1. A landing site where end users can view the newsfeed and track their tasks, etc.
2. An actual personal site which is a site collection created with the URL of the users ID, where users store and share their personal documents

How to create it

To ensure you have the personal site functionality, you are required to have enabled the **User Profile Service Application** in your farm. For detailed configuration steps on how to configure the **User Profile Service Application** refer to the TechNet guide, search TechNet with the following keyword: *Configure My Sites in SharePoint Server 2013*.

Assuming you have configured personal sites on your farm, I'd like to demonstrate a few administrative options which are going to come in handy later. All of these options are available if you have provisioned the **User Profile Service Application** in your farm; in our case we'll call the service application proxy *UserProfileServiceApp*.

1. From the home page of you SharePoint Central Administration click **Manage service applications** located under the **Application Management** group
2. Find the **UserProfileServiceApp** (in your case it might be called differently) and click

Overview of major collaboration components in SharePoint 2013

on the link

3. Among the variety of configuration options, some of which we'll take a look at further, scroll down to the **My Site Settings** group and click **Setup My Sites**

4. From the options available on this page let's take a look at few below:

    a. **Preferred Search Center** is the URL of the search center which will be used when users start their search from the search box located on their personal site. The recommendation is to keep it the same as the main search center, and in our case (as described in Enterprise Search Center) that's a dedicated managed path **/search** under the root site

    b. **My Site Host location** allows you to specify the host where your personal sites will be created. This isn't an independent setting which you can change without consequences. The location of the host must actually exist as another web application with its corresponding IIS website. It's usually recommended to have personal sites created under their own dedicated web application, since security on personal sites is a bit more relaxed and you may want to institute specific monitoring on user's personal sites to ensure governance.

    c. **Site Naming Format** allows you to choose from the several different naming conventions of how your end users sites are named. Typically the URL follows the structure *http://servername/personal/[userId]*. That's because it's the default configuration option. In large organizations this can cause naming conflicts, to avoid this, you can chose several other options to fit your needs

         i. User name (resolve conflicts by using domain_username)
         ii. Domain and user name (will not have conflicts)

    d. **Read Permission Level** is the option allowing you to chose who can access end user's personal sites. By default SharePoint assumes that everyone should have at least the ability to read other users content. Hence, this option is configured to have the **everyone** security group by default. In case you want only users to be able to access their own personal site, or maybe some other special group too, you can leverage the option here to assign those rights

    e. **Security Trimming Options** is an option which is related to the newsfeed content being created as users generate activity on the site. Let's say some-one is following your activity and sees documents you are creating. Among the harmless few documents you have been working on there's a confidential document, and as you interact with it, you generate newsfeed announcements related to it. This option here will allow you to hide or show the activity feed based on security permissions. It's options are:

   i. **Check all links for permission** – don't show activity feed items if the user has no access to the particular document

   ii. **Check only specified links for permission -** don't show activity feed items if the user has no access to the particular document, only those documents which reside in a particular site hierarchy

   iii. **Show all links regardless of permission** – show all the activity links regardless of permission

f. **Privacy Settings** this option allows you to completely open up all of the profile information to the rest of users. By default, only some information is shared with everyone and other information is shared with specific groups, such as colleagues, etc.

The above configuration options will let you chose the behavior of the site, once it's created. Next, let's take a look at how you can manage content on your personal site.

How to manage its content

When you click the **Newsfeed** icon on the home page of your root site, you will be taken to a generic page available to everyone who is viewing the personal site. The reason why this page is personalized to you is because web parts on the page retrieve your username and specific information such as your name, photo, etc. to present on the page.

Any changes made to this site will be reflected on everyone's personal pages; hence the simplified editing experience (**Gear Menu | Edit Page**) is disabled, but the page can be edited in other ways, which we'll discuss later.

Let's take a look at some of the key pages on the personal site:

Overview of major collaboration components in SharePoint 2013

1. The home page of the site displays the quick launch with your photo on it, if it has been uploaded. When clicked, you will have a link to edit your profile, and this includes: uploading your picture and changing variety of other properties that are stored in the user profile database. Among basic information, you can also change the preferences and notification options when someone mentions you on their feed, etc. This can be done by clicking the ellipsis as shown below, and selecting the **Newsfeed Settings**

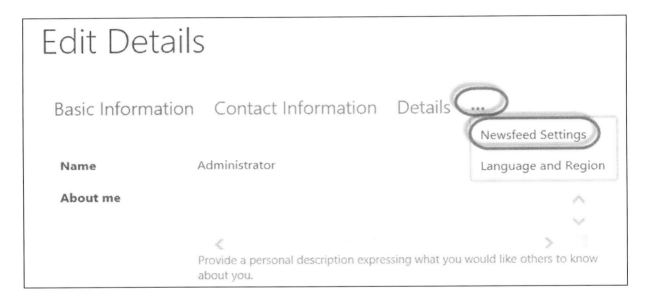

Figure 2.8.1 Newsfeed settings

When you return back to the **Newsfeed**, you will also be able to share updates and review mentions, updates, etc.

2. Your Personal site will appear when you click on **Tasks** link on the quick launch. Also, **Site Contents** on the quick launch; or the **Gear Menu** and select **Site Contents**. If the personal site has not been created for the first time, this will take a moment since the site will be created as a dedicated site collection. The personal site will hold your information such as tasks, documents, etc. By being a dedicated site collection, the administrator will have the granularity of control on how the site is used as well as separating the information between your site and other user sites. You can manage content on the site in a similar fashion as you interact with task lists and documents on other sites. The only exception is editing the home page of the site. Although the

home page and other pages on your personal site are only going to be changed for your username, if you were to change them, there is a special way to modify them which we'll take a look at further. The reason behind this is to ensure that all of the user personal sites follow the same structure and unless decided by the administrator, are not changed beyond recognition.

Overview of major collaboration components in SharePoint 2013

2.9 How does it all fit together

So far we've talked about many of the site templates and how they interact together in various collaboration scenarios. There are a few site templates with similar functionality and components, where others are completely different. You can certainly mix and match various site templates depending on how they serve your needs.

Now, let's take a look at a few examples of how the sites above can be put together into a structure serving a variety of functions. The idea here is for you to take a look at the structure below and borrow those concepts, if appropriate, to apply to your organization.

Again, these are examples, and typically to build an information architecture for a large portal solution you would involve an information architect who assesses the needs of the business and translates those business constructs into sites and sub sites, etc.

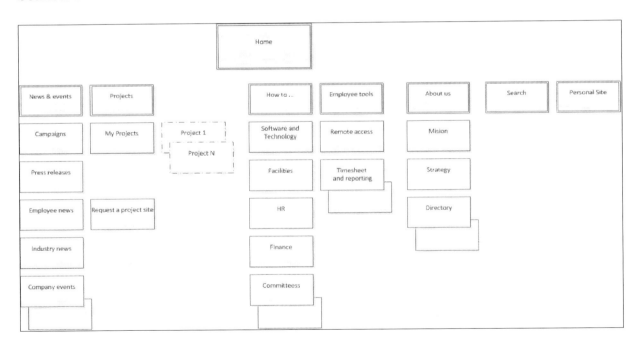

Figure 2.9.1 Example site 1 information architecture

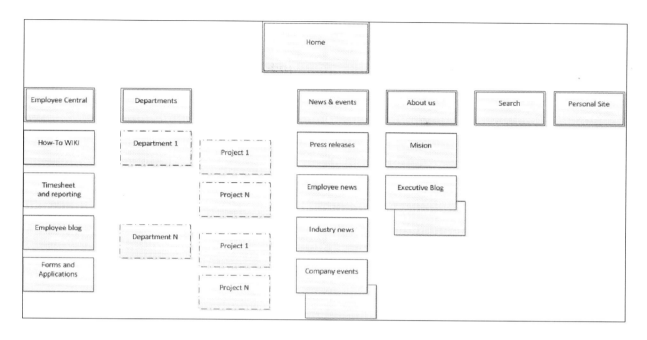

Figure 2.9.2 Example site 2 information architecture

Overview of major collaboration components in SharePoint 2013

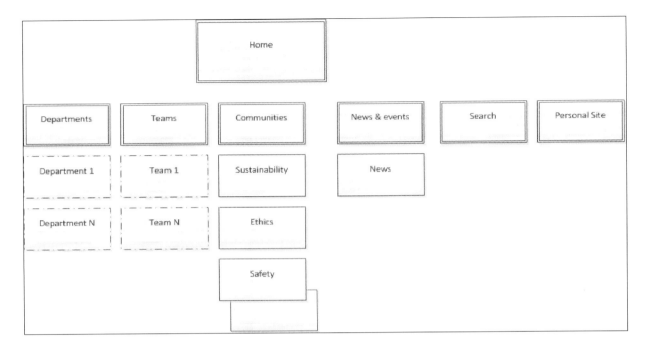

Figure 2.9.3 Example site 3 information architecture

Having sample information architecture references above is great; but this book isn't just about sample reference diagrams. Next, we'll take a look at how you accomplish many common tasks on a typical project where you're tasked with the design and development of a collaboration portal. We'll start with the branding task and see how you apply a corporate look and feel to various templates in a SharePoint 2013 site. Having branding out of the way, we'll take a look at how you can customize common collaboration components so your SharePoint site fits your scenario. Finally, we'll take a look at how you can package the entire solution and automate its deployment to your company's test and production environments.

CHAPTER 3

Applying branding to the collaboration components

In this chapter:

- Setting up and understanding your development environment
- The basics: Changing the look and feel of your SharePoint collaboration sites
- Creating a SharePoint 2013 custom look for collaboration sites
- Working with a SharePoint 2013 master page
- Applying a new SharePoint collaboration site master page
- Adding interaction to your site by extending a SharePoint master page
- Applying a custom user interface to a SharePoint collaboration site
- The basics: Changing the look and feel of SharePoint publishing sites
- Provisioning and applying your own custom page layouts
- Working with search site master page
- The basics: Changing the look and feel of Personal Site
- Changing the look and feel of Personal Sites for individual users
- Putting it all together: automated installation of your branding package to multiple environments

3.1 Setting up and understanding your development environment

Before we get started with SharePoint 2013 branding, I want to make sure we're all looking at the "same screen".

Since in many examples of this book we're going to be working with SharePoint 2013 professional development tools like Visual Studio, and advanced user tools like SharePoint Designer, I am not going to assume you have an infrastructure team which has the development environment set up for you. The easiest and simplest way to get started with SharePoint 2013 customization is to have a pre-built virtualized environment with as many tools set up as possible.

Over the years, there have been at least a few companies which provide virtualized SharePoint environments in the cloud, and my favorite is CloudShare since it has a SharePoint 2013 developer system ready for you to start up and get to work. I recommend you check out the offering from CloudShare.

Now that you have a development environment, whether local or in the cloud, let's take a look at some of the tools which will simplify your life:

1. Mozilla Firefox with the Firebug plug-in. I can't imagine anyone doing user interface development without Firebug; it's too bad that it doesn't run on all of the other browsers. Many other browsers have their own developer toolbars (which you can normally call up by pressing F12) but the richness of features you get with Firebug, in my opinion, is greater. I do, however, recommend downloading other browsers to ensure your customizations run smoothly for your users.

2. Notepad++ is a great tool which you should download. Essentially it's a developer version of a text editor. It's quite useful if you want to edit an ASPX or XML (or any other format) document without editing it in Visual Studio. It gives you some nice features and is very fast. It also recognizes markup of many languages, so it's easier to read CSS or JavaScript in it.

3. CKS: Development Tools Edition is a community extension to Visual Studio 2010 which can be downloaded online. The extension package can be installed using the standard Visual Studio UI; the process is explained on the site where you

download the package. CKS Dev significantly helps with the development process for SharePoint 2013 in Visual Studio 2010. You get templates for various branding and back-end artifacts, which saves time. In this book I will not assume you're running CK S Dev, but if you are, be sure to read the documentation on the tool to see how a few things we have done manually here can be sped up.

As I go through the scenarios, I will mention other resources as they become appropriate. SharePoint has many free and community components which have been developed by community leads. I recommend checking once in a while at www.codeplex.com and searching for "SharePoint"—you will be surprised how many great tools are there.

To create our SharePoint solutions, we'll be mostly using Visual Studio. Visual Studio has a few SharePoint project templates which automate and simplify the creation of SharePoint specific project items.

When a Visual Studio solution is packaged, it produces a **SharePoint Solution Package**. This package defines where various elements of the solution are going to be installed. Some SharePoint elements will be provisioned into the SharePoint database and others will reside on the file system. Depending on the type of the project item added to a Visual Studio solution, its final destination (server file system or a particular SharePoint database) will be defined.

Here is the schematic view of how Visual Studio solutions consist of

Applying branding to the collaboration components

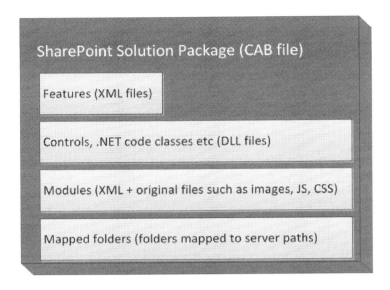

Figure 3.1.1 SharePoint Solution Package components

Let's take a quick look at those components:

- Features – are essentially XML files responsible for a single or a set of SharePoint project items, such as lists, web part definitions, etc. Items for which features are responsible are going to be provisioned to the SharePoint database and surface in the SharePoint user interface as custom functionality, aka a Feature. Where those project items are going to surface in the SharePoint UI will be determined by their features **Scope**. Available scopes are: site feature, web feature, web application and a farm feature. Also, depending on the project item added to a feature, it will appear at pre-defined place in SharePoint. For example, web part definitions will appear as available web parts to be added to pages; whereas lists and libraries will appear as you would expect. All you have to worry about is what project item you need, and the **Feature** framework will take care of the rest.

- Controls, .NET code etc. You can add classes to a Visual Studio solution representing controls, workflows, web part code, events, etc. Some Visual Studio project items will come with accompanying code and Feature elements, such as web parts. Since web parts need .NET code to operate, they need a .NET class; they also need a registration XML to be installed and made available in the SharePoint UI. Your code will be compiled and packaged as a DLL at the time of the Visual Studio solution packaging.

- Modules –represent items which will live in the SharePoint database, in lists and libraries. Modules consist of an actual file, such as an image, a JavaScript file, etc. and an XML file defining into which library those files will be placed. Modules will be added to a feature and the feature will perform the act of copying the dependent files upon its installation/activation.

- Mapped folders – SharePoint doesn't keep all the files in the database. Some files, such as images and user controls are added to the file system so they can be accessed easier using a virtual path. Mapped folders are mapped to an actual SharePoint system folder on the file system and any content you add to it in Visual Studio will be automatically added to the corresponding file system folder at the time of solution deployment. Mapped folders are not tied to features.

- SharePoint Solution Package – each time you build and package your Visual Studio SharePoint solution, you will receive a file (*.WSP). This file is understood by the SharePoint system as an installation file and SharePoint knows how to interpret it's XML to install all of the remaining components we discussed above. Solution packages can be installed right from within Visual Studio, or using scripts and the command line.

Now that we've got a bit of theory about SharePoint Solution Packages, let's build one. We'll start with a simple set of packages allowing us to change the SharePoint user interface and then move on to more complicated packages allowing us to build more complex SharePoint components.

Applying branding to the collaboration components

3.2 The basics: Changing the look and feel of your SharePoint collaboration sites

Scenario

A custom look and feel and design is the requirement that will be either implied or specified. One thing's for sure, you need it, because nobody likes to see vanilla interfaces; everyone's used to the beautiful and interactive Internet. SharePoint has a set of tools and rules related to how you can apply your custom branding. Understanding those tools and rules will ensure that the branding you're going to apply will not break the scalability and upgradability of your site. In here, we'll take a look at some of the basics related to branding of SharePoint collaboration sites.

This part of the book will give you all the details on how you can modify collaboration sites in SharePoint 2013 include:

- Team Sites
- Community Sites
- Project Sites

Set up

Navigate to the instance of the Team Site you created earlier, in case of our virtual environment its URL is *http://sp2013*. To check out how to create it, see *Team Site | How to create it* earlier in the book.

Details

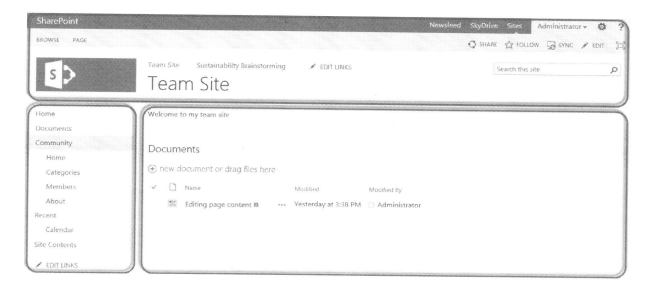

Figure 3.2.1 Team site layout structure

The three areas you see highlighted in the image above are the:

- **Header**—This area exposes the top navigation controls and the title of the site. You also see the controls that allow management of the site, such as the **Gear Menu** menu and ribbon tabs. Those controls will only appear if the user has valid permissions to edit the page or manage the site

- **Left Navigation**—The items that appear in this control can be managed from the administrative user interface and by default those will automatically populate, depending on the lists and document libraries present on the site

- **Content section**—This section is dedicated to the content of the site. By default, some of the content is already preloaded so that users of a team site have something to start with. This content can be edited, providing that the user has sufficient permission to modify the page

The layout of this page is defined by the out-of-the-box master page. The master page is a file that defines the header of the page and a few other elements you see on the page; we'll look at those elements later in the book. Master pages drive the look and feel of each

Applying branding to the collaboration components

page layout that uses it. Custom and out-of-the-box master pages reside in the master page gallery. To access the gallery from the SharePoint interface:

1. Ensure you're logged in to the site with sufficient permissions to manage it.
2. From the home page of existing Team Site instance, *http://sp2013*, click the **Gear Menu | Site Settings**.
3. Under the section **Web Designer Galleries**, click **Master pages and page layouts**.

By default, SharePoint 2013 comes with several out-of-the-box master pages among which you will see *Seattle.master* used by the SharePoint 2013 team site.
Some of the items rendered on the out-of-the-box master page can be toggled on and off. One of them is managing the availability of the quick launch. Here is how you can remove the quick launch options for site users:

1. Click the **Gear Menu | Site Settings**
2. Under **Look and Feel** click **Tree View**
3. Uncheck **Enable Quick Launch** and click **OK**

Now, from the **Look and Feel** section of **Site Settings**, click **Top Link Bar**. This setting will allow you to create a top menu for the site. The information entered here will be saved in the SharePoint database and rolled up in the user controls defined in the master page of a Team Site. As you can see, there is another user control allowing you to do just that, available right on the top of the page with the link titled **Edit Links**.

Apart from structural customizations, you may want to change the color scheme. The SharePoint 2013 user interface is composed out of building blocks: menus, header, body text, etc. You can define the color scheme for those building blocks in a declarative way. We'll take a look at how you can declare a new color scheme, also known as a **Theme**, in the next scenario: *Creating a SharePoint 2013 custom look for collaboration sites*.

SharePoint combines the master page, the theme, optional background images and custom font definitions into what's known as the **Site Look**.

Let's take a look at how you can apply one of the existing site looks onto our team site:

1. Click the **Gear Menu | Site Settings**

2. Under the **Look and Feel** click **Change the look**

The above user interface allows you to choose colors, fonts, and related images that will be used on the site. Select any look of your choice and SharePoint will allow you to adjust colors and fonts for the look, as well as pick a master page to which this look will be applied. When ready, click **Try it out**, and when done, SharePoint will preview the site with the newly selected look; if you like it you can keep it using the **Yes, keep it** link button.

Later, we'll take a look at how you can create your own packaged look.

Related scenarios

- *Working with a SharePoint 2013 master page*
- *Applying a new SharePoint collaboration site master page*
- *Adding interaction to your site by extending a SharePoint master page*
- *Applying a custom user interface to a SharePoint collaboration site*
- *Creating a SharePoint 2013 custom look for collaboration sites*

3.3 Creating a SharePoint 2013 custom look for collaboration sites

Scenario

As you can see from the previous scenario, by being able to create a SharePoint 2013 site look, you can bundle the structural definitions, the colors, the fonts and even the background image all into one package so users can easily pick it. In this scenario we'll take a look at how you can create your own custom look.

Set Up

Navigate to the instance of the Team Site you have created earlier, in case of our virtual environment its URL is *http://sp2013*. To check out how to create it, see *Team Site | How to create it* earlier in the book.

Before we begin

This scenario will address the logistics of creating a SharePoint 2013 custom look package. A custom look contains things such as master pages, the theme, the background image, etc. Some of those items are trivial enough, such as a background image. Others, such as the master page, are more complicated and deserve more attention. To make things simple, first we'll take a look at how to provision our custom look with out-of-the-box components; in subsequent scenarios we'll see how to create our own custom master pages.

First, when you click **Change the look** on you site, under the **Look and Feel**, you see a dynamic list of available packages. To create a new or delete an existing package, you would manually or automatically access the following list:

1. Click the **Gear Menu | Site Settings**
2. Under **Web Designer Galleries** | click **Composed looks**

In here, each item represents:

1. **Name** – the name of the look
2. **Master Page URL** - the URL of the master page
3. **Theme URL** - optional value for the color scheme
4. **Image URL** – the URL of the background image. This is optional
5. **Font Scheme URL** – the URL of the font specification. This is optional
6. **Display Order** – this is the value of the order in which templates will appear in the list above

You can create a new item right from this list, by clicking the **+ new item**, but we'll take a look at how to create a packaged version of our look with Visual Studio. You will also notice that the items in the list above reference components (the master page, theme, and the image) by URL. Let's take a look at where out-of-the-box and custom master pages reside, as this will become important when we provision new items to those locations.

To access the master page gallery:

1. Click the **Gear Menu | Site Settings**
2. Under **Web Designer Galleries** | click **Master pages**

We'll be using one of the master pages in this gallery as the basis for our development further in the scenario: *Working with a SharePoint 2013 master page*

To access the theme and font gallery:

1. Click the **Gear Menu | Site Settings**
2. Under **Web Designer Galleries** | click **Themes** | select the **15** folder

We'll be using one of the below color schemes in this scenario.

Theme file (*.spcolor) is an XML document which defines various parts of the SharePoint 2013 user interface in descriptive elements. Download one of the **spcolor** files and open it in Notepad++ or Visual Studio.

The code will look similar to below:

Applying branding to the collaboration components

```
<s:colorPalette isInverted="false" previewSlot1="Background
Overlay" previewSlot2="BodyText" previewSlot3="AccentText"
xmlns:s="http://schemas.microsoft.com/sharepoint/">
<s:color name="BodyText" value="444444" />
<s:color name="SubtleBodyText" value="777777" />
<s:color name="StrongBodyText" value="262626" />
<s:color name="DisabledText" value="B1B1B1" />
…
</s:colorPalette>
```

Above, we have a `<s:colorPalette>` node which has a few attributes describing how the color scheme will be previewed to the user.

Each child node, `<s:color>`, describes the type of element, which is SharePoint 2013 specific element, for example, **BodyText**, and the color assigned to this element.

You can't come up with your own elements or change the **value** to anything except the HEX of the valid color. When you add a new **spcolor** file to the library, it will be processed by the SharePoint 2013 theme engine and any unexpected values may cause translation problems. The translation process will create a Style Sheet with appropriate values matching the theme. In other words, SharePoint theme is a user friendly specification and theme engine will take care of the Style Sheet generation based on this specification. Behind the scenes, SharePoint will generate all of the selectors to make the consistent look.

If you need to break the rules and go beyond what's available in the **spcolor** file, you can certainly do so, and we'll take a look at how in the scenario: *Applying a custom user interface to a SharePoint collaboration site*.

Now let's take a look at how to provision a very simple new composed look package.

How it's done

1. Open Visual Studio and create a new project: **File** | **New** | **Project** and pick a template **Templates** | **Visual C#** | **Office/SharePoint** | **SharePoint Solutions** | **SharePoint 2013 Empty Project**

2. Specify *http://sp2013* as your debug URL and choose **Deploy as a farm solution** option

3. In the solution explorer, locate the **Features** folder and right click on it to add a new feature

4. Rename the default **Feature1** to **ProvisionCustomLook** so we can track our items better. This feature will be used to upload our custom theme and create a new look

5. In the solution explorer, right click on the project name and select **Add | New Item**....

6. Select **Module** for an item type and give it the name **Theme**

7. Delete the **Sample.txt** file in the module

8. Navigate to *http://sp2013* logged in as the administrator

9. Click the **Gear Menu | Site Settings** and locate **Themes** under **Web Designer Galleries**.

10. Open the **15** folder | locate the **Palette001.spcolor** and pick **Download a Copy** from the context menu. Save the file to disk. The theme definition you have just downloaded is the default theme used on the team site when you create a new instance of it

11. Add the newly downloaded theme to the Visual Studio **Theme** module by right clicking the **Theme** module | select **Add | Existing Item** | locate the **Palette001.spcolor**

12. Rename the existing file to **CustomTheme.spcolor**

13. To test the linkage between our custom theme (**CustomTheme.spcolor**), open the file in Visual Studio and change the value of the **BodyText** to red, as shown below:

    ```
    <s:color name="BodyText" value=" FF0000" />
    ```

14. Open **Elements.xml** in your **Themes** module in Visual Studio and replace its contents with the following:

```xml
<?xml version="1.0" encoding="utf-8"?>
<Elements xmlns="http://schemas.microsoft.com/sharepoint/">
  <Module Name="Theme" List="116" Url="_catalogs/theme/15">
    <File Path="Theme\CustomTheme.spcolor"
      Type="GhostableInLibrary" Url="CustomTheme.spcolor" />
  </Module>
</Elements>
```

In here, the **Module** and **File** element are describing where the new theme is going to be uploaded. The **List** attribute specifies the theme gallery URL and the **15** folder.

In the **File** element, the URL defines where the theme is uploaded. **GhostableinLibrary** tells SharePoint to create a list item to go with your file when it is added to the library

15. Now let's add a new background image to the solution, this image will be automatically rendered as a semi-transparent background on our pages, all taken care of by the theme engine.

    Download the image background provided in the source code of this scenario under the following path: **CustomLook\Images\CustomLook\ThemeImage.jpg**

16. Add a new mapped folder to our Visual Studio solution where the image will reside. Right click on the Visual Studio project name | select **Add** | **SharePoint "Images" Mapped Folder**. Visual Studio will create a new folder in the hierarchy called Images, and a subfolder in it named after the name of your Visual Studio project, ex. **CustomLook**

17. Right click on the **Images** | **CustomLook** folder | select **Add** | **Existing Item** | pick the **ThemeImage.jpg**. The image will be automatically provisioned to the server file system: **C:\Program Files\Common Files\microsoft shared\Web Server Extensions\15\TEMPLATE\IMAGES\CustomLook**. Which is a SharePoint 2013 reserved file system folder to keep images which need to be accessed throughout the site

18. Now that our solution takes care of deploying the theme and the image, let's add the code to create a new item for it in the **Composed looks** library, otherwise no one will be able to pick a new custom look.

Locate the **Features** folder in your solution and right click on **ProvisionCustomLook** in it. Select, **Add Event Receiver**

19. In the **FeatureActivated** section of the code, replace the commented section with the following code:

```
public override void FeatureActivated(SPFeatureReceiverProperties properties)
{
  SPWeb web = properties.Feature.Parent as SPWeb;
  SPList list = web.Lists["Composed Looks"];

  // Adding a new composed look item
  SPListItem item = list.AddItem();

  // Title of the look
  item["Title"] = "CustomLook";

  // Internal name of the look
  item[new Guid("{bfc6f32c-668c-43c4-a903-847cca2f9b3c}")] = "CustomLook";

  // URL of the out-of-the-box master page
  SPFieldUrlValue masterUrl = new SPFieldUrlValue();
  masterUrl.Url = web.ServerRelativeUrl + "/_catalogs/masterpage/seattle.master";
  masterUrl.Description = web.ServerRelativeUrl + "/_catalogs/masterpage/seattle.master";
  item["MasterPageUrl"] = masterUrl;

  // URL of our custom theme
```

Applying branding to the collaboration components

```
        SPFieldUrlValue themeUrl = new SPFieldUrlValue();
        themeUrl.Url = web.ServerRelativeUrl + "/_catalogs/theme/15/
        CustomTheme.spcolor";
        themeUrl.Description = web.ServerRelativeUrl + "/_catalogs/
        theme/15/CustomTheme.spcolor";
        item["ThemeUrl"] = themeUrl;

        // URL of our background image
        SPFieldUrlValue imageUrl = new SPFieldUrlValue();
        imageUrl.Url = "/_layouts/15/images/CustomLook/ThemeImage.jpg";
        imageUrl.Description = "/_layouts/15/images/CustomLook/ThemeImage.
        jpg";
        item["ImageUrl"] = imageUrl;

        // Optional value for the custom font and display order
        //item["FontSchemeUrl"] = "";
        //item["DisplayOrder"] = 100;
        item.Update();
        web.Dispose();
    }
```

The above functionality of the feature receiver will execute custom .NET code when the solution gets deployed and the feature gets activated. This will create a new list item representing our composed look.

20. Let's deploy the solution; right click the solution name and click **Deploy**

Wait for Visual Studio to finish the solution deployment by following the **Output** windows messages. Navigate back to the site root *http://sp2013* | click the **Gear Menu** | **Change the look** | scroll to the bottom to find our custom composed look named **CustomLook**. From here, you can preview and apply the look and you will see our custom background image added to the background, as well as the red body text.

Related scenarios

- *Working with a SharePoint 2013 master page*
- *Applying a new SharePoint collaboration site master page*
- *Adding interaction to your site by extending a SharePoint master page*
- *Applying a custom user interface to a SharePoint collaboration site*

3.4 Working with a SharePoint 2013 master page

Scenario

In the previous scenario we looked at how to change the colors of the elements of the existing page, largerly defined by the master page. A master page allows for structural modifications on your site pages. Things like, where the navigation will appear or whether it will appear at all, and if the site will have a footer or not. When you need to change the structure available for pages – you turn to the master page. In this scenario, we'll take a look at what are some of the basic elements of the SharePoint collaboration master page. Knowing the main parts of the out-of-the-box master page will help you add your own controls around sections.

Set up

Navigate to the instance of the Team Site you have created earlier, in case of our virtual environment its URL is *http://sp2013.* To check out how to create it, see *Team Site | How to create it* earlier in the book.

Details

If you remember earlier, we talked about the default seattle.master master page used in collaboration sites. Well, in order for us to make structural changes on the collaboration page, such as: moving things around on the page, removing sections on the page, and more, we will have to create an instance of our own master page and assign it to be used on the site instead of the default one.

Once you get the hang of it, you'll be happy to know that almost all of the SharePoint site templates use the same master page at their core. In fact, the following site templates we closely look at use exactly the same master page:

- Publishing Portal
- Team Site
- Community Site

- Project Site
- Enterprise WIKI
- Enterprise Search Center

Before we go and start modifying the new instance of the master page, let's spend some time looking at what's in the v5 master page. Don't get discouraged, poking around the master page is actually the best way to learn it in detail and this is something we'll do in a little bit. Before that, let's look at some of the major components in the master page. Download an instance of the seattle.master from your Team Site:

1. From the *http://sp2013*, click the **Gear Menu | Site Settings**
2. Under the **Web Designer Galleries** click **Master Pages**
3. Download the **seattle.master** to the file system
4. Open the file from the file system in **Visual Studio** or **Notepad++**

First, a high level view of the master page various components and where they are on the page.

Applying branding to the collaboration components

Figure 3.4.1 Detailed master page layout

Next, let's have a more granular look at the master page components. My comments are going to be in bold in the listing below. I will be explaining most of the components on the master page; some items are going to be cut to avoid redundancy. Plus, if you need more granularities in your work, you can poke around the master page with tools like Firebug, which we'll take a look at in a bit.

```
<%@Master language="C#"%> <!--Defining that this file is a master page -->
<%@ Register Tagprefix="SharePoint" … <!-- References library for buttons
and other page controls-->
<%@ Register Tagprefix="Utilities" … <!-- References helper controls -->
<%@ Import Namespace="Microsoft.SharePoint" … <!-- Registers the general
```

```
SharePoint namespace-->
<%@ Assembly Name="Microsoft.Web.CommandUI … <!-- Registers a library to
facilitate the ribbon -->
<%@ Register Tagprefix="WebPartPages" … <!-- Registers a library to
facilitate web part pages -->
<%@ Register TagPrefix="wssuc" … <!-- Registers a user control to display
the welcome menu-->


<!DOCTYPE html PUBLIC … <!-- SharePoint uses the strict doctype-->
<head runat="server">
<!-- ... Truncated section - various page meta elements ... -->
<SharePoint:RobotsMetaTag … <!-- Reserved for backwards compatibility,
performs no function -->


<!-- Page title retrieved and displayed in the browser header-->
<SharePoint:PageTitle runat="server">
      <asp:ContentPlaceHolder id="PlaceHolderPageTitle" runat="server">
          <SharePoint:ProjectProperty Property="Title" runat="server" />
      </asp:ContentPlaceHolder>
</SharePoint:PageTitle>


<!-- Favicon for the site -->
<SharePoint:SPShortcutIcon runat="server" IconUrl="/_layouts/15/images/
favicon.ico" />


<!-- ... Truncated section ... -->
<SharePoint:ScriptLink language="javascript" … <!-- Loading SharePoint
core JavaScript files-->


<!-- ... Truncated section ... -->
```

Applying branding to the collaboration components

```
<!-- This control will inject any custom references to custom CSS and
script -->
<SharePoint:DelegateControl runat="server" ControlId="AdditionalPageHead" …
<!-- ... Truncated section ... -->
</head>
```

So far we've looked at the head section of the page where most utility classes and behind the scenes controls are registered as well as the out-of-the-box and custom scripts and style sheets are loaded. Next, on to the body of the master page.

```
<body>
  <!-- ... Truncated section ... -->


  <!-- Section reserved for global navigation -->
<SharePoint:DelegateControl runat="server" ControlId="GlobalNavigation" />

<!-- ... Truncated section - accessibility controls for screen readers ...
-->
<!-- Suite bar section starts here -->
<div id="suiteBar" class="ms-dialogHidden">
<div class="ms-tableRow">
<div id="suiteBarLeft"> <!--Left part of the suite bar -->


<!-- ... Truncated section … -->
<!--Renders actual links on the left side-->
<SharePoint:SuiteBarBrandingElement runat="server" />


<!--Delegate control to add additional icons to the suite bar -->
<SharePoint:DelegateControl id="ID_SuiteLinksDelegate"
ControlId="SuiteLinksDelegate" runat="server" />
```

```
<!-- Right section of the suite bar is inserted here: Welcome menu, Gear
Menu -->
<div id="suiteBarRight">

<!-- Section of the suite bar for the welcome menu -->
<div id="welcomeMenuBox">
<wssuc:Welcome id="IdWelcome" runat="server" EnableViewState="false" />

<!--Delegate control to add additional icons to the right side of the suite
bar -->
<SharePoint:DelegateControl ControlId="GlobalSiteLink2"
ID="GlobalDelegate2" Scope="Farm" runat="server" />

<!-- ... Truncated section - Gear Menu elements ... -->
<span id="ms-help">
<SharePoint:ThemedClusteredHoverImage runat="server" … <!-- Section
dedicated to help icon -->

<!-- ... Truncated section ... -->
<!-- Section dedicated to ribbon, left section: Page, Browse, other ribbon
tabs; and right section: Share, Follow, Synch, Edit, Other right hand side
ribbon options-->
<div id="s4-ribbonrow">

<!-- ... Truncated section - ribbon hierarchy and controls ... -->
<SharePoint:DeveloperDashboard runat="server" /> <!—Developer dashboard
button if enabled-->

<!-- Controls allowing you to publish the page, check in, check out, etc.
-->
```

```
<SharePoint:DelegateControl runat="server" ControlId="PublishingConsole"
Id="PublishingConsoleDelegate" />
<!-- ... Truncated section - ribbon hierarchy and controls ... -->


<!-- Beginning of the main content area -->
<div id="s4-workspace" class="ms-core-overlay">
<div id="s4-bodyContainer">
<div id="s4-titlerow" class="ms-dialogHidden ms-core-header s4-
titlerowhidetitle">
<div id="titleAreaBox" … <!-- Section below the ribbon but before the
actual content starts -->


<div id="siteIcon" … <!--Site logo-->
<div class="ms-breadcrumb-box … <!-- Breadcrumb section-->


<!-- ... Truncated section - breadcrumb area ... -->
<!-- ... Truncated section - site title section in the header ... -->


<h1 id="pageTitle" class="ms-core-pageTitle">
   <!-- ... Truncated section - site description section in the header -->
<asp:ContentPlaceHolder id="PlaceHolderPageDescription" runat="server" />


<!-- Search box section -->
<div id="searchInputBox">
<SharePoint:DelegateControl runat="server" ControlId="SmallSearchInputBox"
/>
</div>
<div id="contentRow"> <! -- Content begins here -->
<div id="sideNavBox" … <!-- Quick launch on the left of the content area-->
```

```
<!-- … Truncated section - additional links right below the quick launch:
Site Contents, Recycle bin… -->
<div id="contentBox" … <!-- Center content area-->
<div id="notificationArea" class="ms-notif-box"></div> … <!--Area for "in
progress" messages -->
<!-- Page status bar : published, check in, etc. -->
<div id="pageStatusBar"></div>


<!-- Section to inject page layout for publishing pages, if applicable -->
<a name="mainContent" tabindex="-1"></a>
<asp:ContentPlaceHolder id="PlaceHolderMain" runat="server" />


<!--Truncated section, unused placeholders which are hidden-->
</body>
```

That's it; we've skimmed through the main structure of the typical collaboration master page. As promised, right after the next section, we're going to take a look at how to discover more granular parts of the master page using various tools like IE Developer Toolbar and Firebug.

Using browser developer tools you can significantly increase your productivity during master page customization and actually preview your changes before applying them to Visual Studio and waiting for a longer deployment process to confirm that your changes actually work as expected. Below is a snapshot of a SharePoint Team site being modified where we preview the background color of the title area on the fly (color changed to #0072C6)

Applying branding to the collaboration components

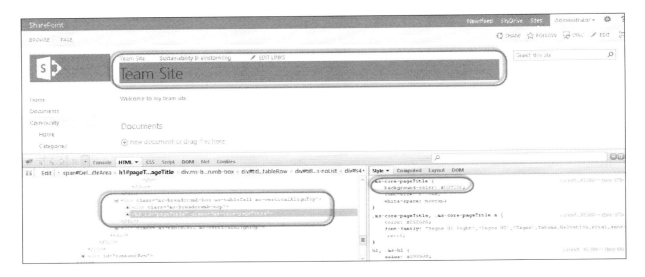

Figure 3.4.1 Previewing stylesheet changes at run time

Related scenarios

- Applying a new SharePoint collaboration site master page
- Adding interaction to your site by extending a SharePoint master page
- Applying a custom user interface to a SharePoint collaboration site

3.5 Applying a new SharePoint collaboration site master page

Scenario

As we've seen in the previous scenario, a master page is a powerful concept allowing you to make structural changes to the site. Next on the agenda is to see how we can set the new master page as a current master page on the site. We'll use a Visual Studio solution for this.

Set up

I'm assuming you have an existing instance of the Team Site you have created earlier. Also, you will require Visual Studio 2012 installed in your development environment. If you're using a pre-created SharePoint 2013 development environment from CloudShare, you're all ready to go. For more information on how to get Visual Studio 2012 on your environment, search for *Installing Visual Studio MSDN*.

How it's done

Let's take a look at what's involved in creating a Visual Studio solution which installs and sets a new master page on the site:

1. Open Visual Studio and create a new project: **File | New | Project** and pick a template **Templates | Visual C# | Office/SharePoint | SharePoint Solutions | SharePoint 2013 Empty Project**

2. Specify *http://sp2013* as your debug URL and choose **Deploy as a farm solution** option

3. In the solution explorer, locate the **Features** folder and right click on it to add a new feature

4. Rename the default **Feature1** to **ProvisionCollabMaster** so we can track our items better. This feature will be used to upload our custom master page to the gallery

Applying branding to the collaboration components

5. In the solution explorer, right click on the project name and select **Add | New Item**....

6. Select **Module** for an item type and give it the name **Masterpage**

7. Rename the **Sample.txt** file in the module to **newmaster.master**

8. Navigate to http://sp2013 logged in as administrator

9. Click the **Gear Menu | Site Settings** and locate **Masterpages** under **Web Designer Galleries**.

10. Locate the **seattle.master** and pick **Download a Copy** from the context menu. Save the file to disk. The master page you have just downloaded is the default master page used on the team site when you create new instance of it

11. Open the newly downloaded master page in Visual Studio and copy its content to the **newmaster.master** we just created. Let's also add a piece of customization to our new master page, locate the following in the code of **newmaster.master** (the default logo of the team site):

    siteIcon.png

    and replace it with:

    SiteCollections_48.png

    This custom string replaces the logo of the site with another SharePoint image which will help us easily identify that our custom master page has been applied to the site

12. Open the **Elements.xml** in your master page module in Visual Studio and replace its contents with the following:

```
<?xml version="1.0" encoding="utf-8"?>
<Elements xmlns="http://schemas.microsoft.com/sharepoint/">
  <Module Name="MasterPage" List="116" Url="_catalogs/masterpage">
    <File Path="MasterPage\newmaster.master"
Type="GhostableInLibrary" Url="newmaster.master" />
```

```xml
    </Module>
</Elements>
```

In here, the **Module** and **File** elements are describing where the new master page is going to be uploaded. The **List** attribute specifies the master page gallery URL.

In the **File** element, the URL defines where the master page is uploaded. **GhostableInLibrary** tells SharePoint to create a list item to hold metadata for your file when it is added to the library. Each of such files will live in the SharePoint content database.

13. Now that our solution takes care of deploying the master page, let's add the code to set the master page as a current on the site, otherwise SharePoint will keep using **seattle.master**.
    Locate the **Features** folder in your solution and right click on **ProvisionCollabMaster** in it. Select, **Add Event Receiver**

14. In the **FeatureActivated** section of the code, replace the commented section with the following code:

```csharp
public override void FeatureActivated(SPFeatureReceiverProperties properties)
{
    SPWeb web = properties.Feature.Parent as SPWeb;
    web.CustomMasterUrl = "/_catalogs/masterpage/newmaster.master";
    web.MasterUrl = "/_catalogs/masterpage/newmaster.master";
    web.Update();
    web.Dispose();
}
```

The above functionality of the feature receiver will execute custom .NET code when the solution gets deployed and the feature gets activated. This will set our custom master page as the current site master page.

15. Let's deploy the solution; right click the solution name and click **Deploy**

Applying branding to the collaboration components

Wait for Visual Studio to finish the solution deployment by following the **Output** windows messages. Navigate back to the site root *http://sp2013* to see that the logo of the site has changed to another image.

Related scenarios

- *Adding interaction to your site by extending a SharePoint master page*

3.6 Adding interaction to your site by extending a SharePoint master page

Scenario

In the previous scenario we looked at how to take an existing out-of-the-box master page and customize a small part of it just to see that our master page has been applied. In the spirit of exploration, let's make another customization to our master page and this time a bit more complex and useful. Let's make a customization allowing users to show or hide the site header which should give users more space to view libraries and content on the site. This is especially useful when users are going to view the page on their tablet. We'll also see how you can save a user preference so next time the site loads, it either shows or hides the site header depending on the previous selection our user has made.

Set up

This is a bit more complex customization since it will involve using JavaScript and the jQuery library.

To keep things simple, we're going to reuse the same solution structure we have used in the above scenario, since it already has all of the necessary artifacts: master page and provisioning code.

How it's done

1. In Visual Studio, open the **Masterpage** you created earlier and containing **newmaster.master**

2. In your **newmaster.master** locate the following piece of code:
   ```
   <div id="contentRow">
   ```
   add the code below, immediately before the `<div id="contentRow">`

   ```
   <div id="hide-header-link">
       <img src="/_layouts/15/images/ARRUPA.gif" alt="hide header"
   ```

Applying branding to the collaboration components

```
            onclick="hideHeader();" />
    </div>
    <div id="show-header-link" style="display:none">
        <img src="/_layouts/15/images/ARRDOWNA.gif" alt="show header"
        onclick="showHeader();"/>
    </div>
```

The code above is just two images: arrow up and arrow down; they will both call a JavaScript function we're about to add to show or hide the site header.

3. In your **newsmaster.master** locate the following code

   ```
   </head>
   ```

   Add the two script references below, immediately before it:

   ```
   <script src="/_layouts/15/CustomBranding/jquery.js" type="text/javascript"></script>
   <script src="/_layouts/15/CustomBranding/CustomBrandingScripts.js" type="text/javascript"></script>
   ```

   Those scripts don't exist yet, we'll add them next.

4. In your Visual Studio solution, right click on the project name and from the context menu select **Add | SharePoint "Layouts" Mapped Folder**

5. Locate the **Layouts** folder that has been just created in your Visual Studio solution and the folder below it. Rename the folder below it to **CustomBranding**

6. Right click on the **CustomBranding** folder | select **Add | New Item ...** | pick **Web** category on the left | select **JavaScript File** from the list | provide **CustomBrandingScripts.js** as the file name

7. Add the following code to the newly created JavaScript file

```javascript
function hideHeader() {
    $('#s4-titlerow').hide('slow');
    $('#show-header-link').show('fast');
    $('#hide-header-link').hide('fast');
    setCookie("CustomHeader", "hide", 100);
}

function showHeader() {
    $('#s4-titlerow').show('slow');
    $('#show-header-link').hide('fast');
    $('#hide-header-link').show('fast');
    deleteCookie("CustomHeader");
}

function setCookie(name, value, days) {
    if (days) {
        var date = new Date();
        date.setTime(date.getTime() + (days * 24 * 60 * 60 * 1000));
        var expires = "; expires=" + date.toGMTString();
    }
    else var expires = "";
    document.cookie = name + "=" + value + expires + "; path=/";
}

function getCookie(name) {
    var nameEQ = name + "=";
    var ca = document.cookie.split(';');
    for (var i = 0; i < ca.length; i++) {
        var c = ca[i];
        while (c.charAt(0) == ' ') c = c.substring(1, c.length);
```

```
            if (c.indexOf(nameEQ) == 0) return c.substring(nameEQ.length,
c.length);
    }
    return null;
}


function deleteCookie(name) {
    setCookie(name, "", -1);
}



function setHeaderState() {
    if (getCookie("CustomHeader") != null) {
        $('#s4-titlerow').hide();
        $('#show-header-link').show();
        $('#hide-header-link').hide();
    }
}
```

The above code uses jQuery to hide or show the header based on a specific function called irrespective of whether the user clicked the **hide** or **show** image button. Additionally, user preferences are saved into a web cookie and when a user loads the site next, their preferences are respected.

8. Since we're using jQuery to help us with the hide/show effect, let's get the latest copy of jQuery at *http://jquery.com*. Once you download the file, save it as jquery.js since that's how it's referenced in our masterpage.

9. Right click on the CustomBranding folder | select Add | Existing Item … | pick the jquery.js you downloaded

10. Deploy the solution with Visual Studio and navigate to your team site, *http://sp2013*. You will see the header show/hide images as shown below:

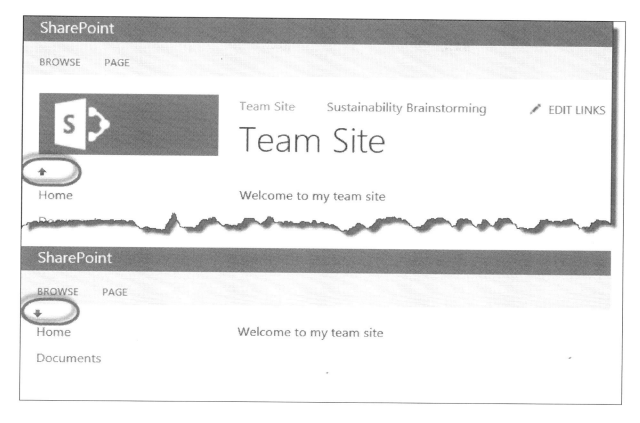

Figure 3.6.1 Show/Hide site header functionality added to the master page

Final Notes

In essence, this scenario is one of the most important, since each site in SharePoint has a master page and that's the place you turn to make global user interface customizations. When I say global, this means that your customizations will appear for a given team site and any page on that team site including system pages such as the **Site Settings** page. Sites created underneath a team site (aka Team Site children) may have a different master page set for them.

By all means you may not need such a global customization, you may require the customization to appear only on a given page and so on; and that's possible, we'll take a look at how to do just that over the next few scenarios.

Applying branding to the collaboration components

Related scenarios

- *Applying a new SharePoint collaboration site master page*

3.7 Applying a custom user interface to a SharePoint collaboration site

Scenario

You're now armed with the knowledge around where the site master page is and what are some of the tools available in SharePoint to apply custom site branding. Now let's take a look at what is the typical process involved in applying a custom user interface on a SharePoint collaboration site.

Set up

We'll use exactly the same team site and Visual Studio solution as in the previous scenario, to keep things simple. You'll also need Firebug, a tool I mentioned earlier available in the Firefox browser to help you preview your branding before it'll go into Visual Studio.

Lastly, we'll be using a pre-created HTML markup which accompanies this book's source code, so make sure you download the source code for the sample site; the next section explains exactly where to find this sample site source code.

How it's done

In the downloadable source code of this book, you will find a sub folder called SampleSite. This folder will have an HTML page, a style sheet, and few images in a separate folder. If you open the HTML page, you will see it looks like the home page of a typical collaboration site with a header, a few menus, and a main content area. This type of a cut up is something you will receive from a design agency tasked with designing your site. The design agency won't typically know how to apply your branding to a SharePoint site, so they'll give you a static cut up like this to get started with. And that's how we'll get started with it too.

Next, we're going to see how you can use popular developer tools such as Firebug or the IE Developer toolbar to discover granular elements of our master page and learn how those can help you apply your custom markup to the site.

I'm going to reuse the same solution I have used all along in this scenario. I will keep the

Applying branding to the collaboration components

master page as **newmaster.master** and for the style sheet I will use **branding.css**. To add a style sheet to your Visual Studio solution:

1. In your Visual Studio solution locate the **CustomBranding** folder, under the **Layouts** folder created earlier
2. Right click on the **CustomBranding** folder | select **Add** | **New Item ...** | pick **Web** category on the left | select **Style Sheet** from the list | provide **branding.css** as the file name
3. Click **Add**
4. Open **newmaster.master** in Visual Studio, locate the `</head>` in it's markup and add the following reference to **branding.css** right before the `</head>`:

```
<link rel="StyleSheet" href="/_layouts/15/CustomBranding/branding.css" type="text/css" media="screen">
```

Ensure the **newmaster.master** is deployed to the site, if you skipped over the scenario: *Applying a new SharePoint collaboration site master page*. Once the solution has been deployed with Visual Studio, open the site and view the source of the page in the browser. Search for the reference **branding.css** in the source. If you can find it, you know that our custom master page and style sheet are applied.

From here, I will be using Firebug from Firefox, which requires your site to run in Firefox; you can install Firefox and Firebug in your virtual machine environment. You can also use the IE Developer Toolbar by pressing F12 while your site is open in the browser.

Let's first take a look at the markup of the sample page which was included in our sample HTML markup:

1. Open the HTML page within the SampleSite in either Visual Studio or Notepad++
2. Let's take a look at the markup of the page:

```
<body>
<header id="header">
<div class="topSection">
```

```
        <div id="logo">
        </div>
        <ul>
                <li>Employee Central</li>
                <li>Departments</li>
                <li>News & Events</li>
                <li>About us</li>
        </ul>
</div>
</header>

<article>
<div id="container">
        <div id="rightNav">
                <ul>
                        <li><a>Home</a></li>
                        <li><a>Documents</a></li>
                        <li><a>Site Contents</a></li>
                </ul>
        </div>
</div>
</article>
</body>
```

This markup is way too simple for us to just copy and paste to our SharePoint site, so we'll have to do a bit of fitting in to make things happen. In fact most of the work will have to be done on the style sheet to adjust the out-of-the-box SharePoint look and feel to how we need it to look.

Let's take a look at what needs to be done from the schematic standpoint before we dig into details:

Applying branding to the collaboration components

1. What we'll refer to as the **suite bar**, which is the area holding the links such as the **Newsfeed**, **SkyDrive**, **Sites**, etc, will need to go inside our header in a designated section on the right, allocated for tools

Figure 3.7.1 Changes to suite bar

2. The ribbon tabs such as **Browse** and **Page** will then become the top area of the page. By default users see the **Browse** section of the page as they navigate through the site, this section will contain our custom header. When users choose the **Page** ribbon tab – our custom header will be replaced with a ribbon bar allowing users to work with the page, etc. Same goes for document libraries, etc.

Figure 3.7.2 SharePoint ribbon still present while working with the page

3. What we'll refer to as the **breadcrumb**, which is a set of links users can add, will be sitting right below the logo in the header of our site. This will allow users to build up their own top navigation bar. Conceptually, it's not a traditional breadcrumb, but that's how it's referred to in a SharePoint master page and we'll stick to that reference to make this easier to follow

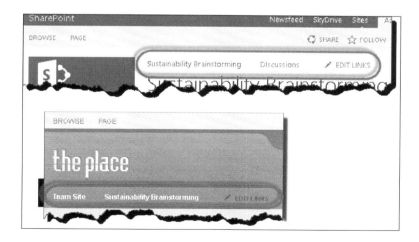

Figure 3.7.3 Breadcrumb positioning

Applying branding to the collaboration components

4. The search box will sit in the header as well in the right hand side of the page, which is a pretty typical location for a collaboration site search box. That's the last element of the header

5. The main body area will have a bit of padding on both sides to focus users more on the content. We'll add a bit of a custom coloring to the main area to make it stand out

6. The left navigation will remain as-is but we'll spice it up with rounded corners and a bit of shadow to make it more modern

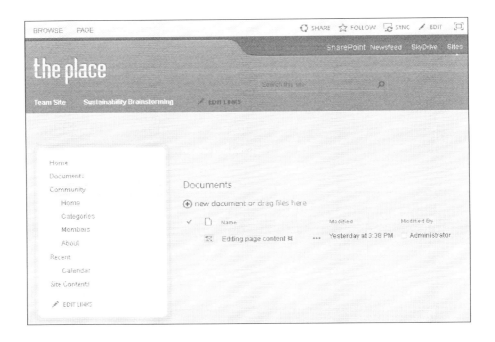

Figure 3.7.4 Overall target site look

That's great, so how do we get there? We'll start with making structural customizations to our site which will go into the master page. The only structural modification has to do with the **suite bar** (#1 in the list above). By default the suite bar is the top bar on the page and we need to go into our header. From the markup perspective, it's easily visible using Firebug or the IE Developer Tool bar

Chapter 3

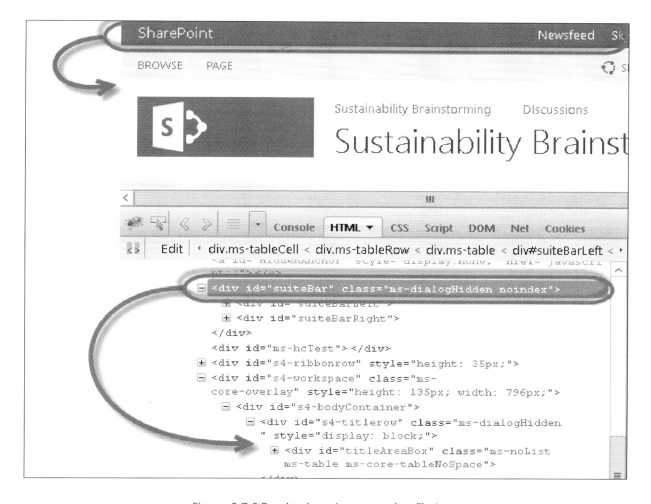

Figure 3.7.5 Previewing changes using Firebug

Let's move it into the header section of the master page:

1. In your Visual Studio locate and open to edit the **newmaster.master**
2. Locate the following markup representing the beginning of the suite bar:

    ```
    <div id="suiteBar" class="ms-dialogHidden noindex">
    ```

3. Select and copy the entire section representing the suite bar and place it right

Applying branding to the collaboration components

underneath the following declaration so it's inside the DIV:

```
<div id="s4-titlerow" class="ms-dialogHidden s4-titlerowhidetitle">
```

That's really the only structural customization we'll make.

Next by using Firebug or the IE Developer toolbar we'll be going through the existing team site page to see which sections need to have different properties to match our look and feel. The below listing assumes you will be working with Visual Studio, but feel free to find the selectors referenced with Firebug and change their properties to preview the results before everything gets entered in Visual Studio.

Let's now open our **branding.css** and ensure that our SharePoint styles look like we need them to:

1. First we'll reset all of the SharePoint defaults to the styles we need by adding the following code:

    ```css
    body, ul{
        font-size: 12px;
        color: #fff;
        font-family: Arial,Helvetica,sans-serif;
        padding:0;
        margin:0;
        list-style:none;}
    ```

2. Next we'll make the minimal width of the page for 1024 resolution by adding the following to our **branding.css:**

    ```css
    #s4-bodyContainer{min-width:1024px;}
    ```

3. Then we'll adjust our background color to light grey:

    ```css
    #s4-workspace{background-color:#ededed;}
    ```

4. Now onto the header. The **s4-titlerow** section in the master page denotes the area that holds the out-of-the-box ribbon and the header section with it's logo, the nav, etc. Since our header is broken down into two pieces, we'll define those and their positioning next by adding the following code:

```
#s4-titlerow{
    height: 140px;
    padding: 0;
    background:url(/_layouts/15/images/CustomBranding/header-2.jpg) repeat-x;
    position:relative;}
#s4-titlerow #titleAreaBox{
    height: 140px;
    padding: 0 70px 0 70px;
    margin: 0;
    background:url(/_layouts/15/images/CustomBranding/header-1.jpg) no-repeat;}
```

5. You'll notice we added two images but we haven't added them to our solution. Let's do that next by right clicking on the **project** folder | **Add** | **SharePoint "Images" Mapped Folder**

6. Add a **CustomBranding** sub folder under the images mapped folder

7. Right click on the **CustomBranding** | select **Add** | **Existing Item …** | pick the following three files provided in the **SampleSite** | **images**:

    a. Header-1
    b. Header2
    c. Logo

8. Click **Add** to add them all

Applying branding to the collaboration components

9. Next we adjust the boundaries of our site logo - "the place" by adding the following code to the style sheet:

```
#s4-titlerow #siteIcon{
    height: 51px;
    width: 131px;
    float: left;
    margin-top: 35px;
    position:absolute;}
```

10. Since we have a logo and don't need the title of the site we can hide it here:

```
#pageTitle{
    display: none;}
```

11. Next we'll ensure the breadcrumb and the search box are going to be positioned at the bottom of the header, have a right padding, margins and link color:

```
#s4-titlerow .ms-verticalAlignTop{vertical-align: bottom;}
#s4-titlerow .ms-breadcrumb-box{padding-bottom:12px;}
#s4-titlerow ul, #s4-titlerow a{color: #fff;}
#s4-titlerow #titleAreaRow .ms-breadcrumb-top ul{
    font-weight: bold;}
#s4-titlerow #searchInputBox  {padding-bottom:25px;}
```

12. Remember the suite bar we moved in the master page, we'll now we need to adjust it's positioning and add a bit of transparency so it flows with the colors on the site:

```
#suiteBar{
    float: right;}
#s4-titlerow #suiteBar #suiteBarLeft{background-color:transparent;
padding-top:7px;}
```

13. Now, onto the content area. We'll start by adding a bit of padding to our center area to make it stand out more and make other elements such as the left navigation align properly with the content:

```
#contentRow{
      padding: 40px 70px 0 70px;}
#contentRow #sideNavBox .ms-core-sideNavBox-removeLeftMargin{
margin:0;}
#contentBox{
      margin: 0 0 0 260px;}
#contentRow #sideNavBox .ms-core-sideNavBox-removeLeftMargin{
margin:0;}
```

14. Finally, we'll define width for the left navigation, adding outer shadow to the navigation and making sure it works across most browsers

```
#contentRow #sideNavBox{
      width:230px;
      padding: 4px;
      margin:0;
      box-shadow: 0 0 6px #cacaca;
      border-radius: 10px;
      background-color:#e8e8e8;}
#contentRow #sideNavBox .ms-core-listMenu-root{
      padding: 15px 2px;
      border-radius: 10px;
      background-color:#fff;}
```

15. Great, we're done. Save and deploy your customization to a team site and preview your changes in a browser.

Applying branding to the collaboration components

If you missed a step or two, check out the accompanying source code for this scenario where you can step through our CSS for even more detailed explanations in-line. You can also use a copy of the master page we used to create a replica of what is discussed here.

Related scenarios

- *Adding interaction to your site by extending a SharePoint master page*
- *Applying a new SharePoint collaboration site master page*

3.8 The basics: Changing the look and feel of SharePoint publishing sites

Scenario

Above we looked at how to modify the look and feel of SharePoint collaboration sites and that's the majority of sites we'll be working with in this book. However, as we looked at earlier, SharePoint Publishing sites are often used for several types of sites in collaboration portals; those include the landing area for the portal as well as news & events sites.

A publishing site by its nature has a set of features, also known as the publishing infrastructure, which facilitates more complex branding and scalable site publishing workflows.

Set up

Unlike previous examples, in this scenario we'll be using a Publishing Site, therefore you will need to create a new site collection using the Publishing Site template. To see how you can create new Publishing Site instance check out earlier scenario: *Publishing Portal | How to create it*. For consistency, in this scenario, I'll assume your publishing site has the URL of: *http://sp2013/news*.

Details

Let's take a look at how the branding is structured for publishing sites. Publishing sites still use master pages which defines the header of the page and the main areas on the page. As you already know it's the same master page as in collaboration sites. You can change the master page your site is using, and we'll see how in a moment. You can specify your custom Style Sheet right from the administrative UI, or programmatically, and that's the same for collaboration sites. One of the main differences between the collaboration site and publishing is that each page in a publishing site has the choice of a few out-of-the-box page layouts that it can inherit from.

Page layouts define zones and areas for the page's main body. Each page which inherits from a particular page layout will have zones and areas defined in the page layout. Those zones and other markup will appear on pages just as defined in the page layout which a

Applying branding to the collaboration components

particular page inherits. So in essence, there is another layer of markup definition between the page and a master page and that layer is a page layout.

In the collaboration site template, we had one layout defined in the master page; we also had a few administrative options allowing us to hide the left navigation, for example, or change the order of things. We couldn't, however, add our own custom top navigation menu with slick a UI and the behavior we require. By using a page layout, we can define the look and feel of anything on the page. Page layouts can use additional style sheets to help them govern the look of the page. This additional framework will allow you to make structural changes to individual pages, using the layout as a mediator, while collaboration sites used one master page only and all the pages were governed only by that one master page.

Here is an example of how you can use different page layouts in your solution. The home page of your portal will have a complex structure with multiple zones where different web parts and lists are going to be hosted in. You might also have the news & events page on the site. This page will have the title and body of the news piece and possibly some additional metadata, such as the date of the news release. For each major type of page, or page with separate behavior, you may require a separate page layout.

Alternatively to creating multiple page layouts, you can create a generic layout which covers most cases. However, if you have over five layout requirements, it might complicate the content authoring experience, and your users might be confused about which zone they should then use for which content. Page layouts can also be used to tie content to a different **content type**. A content type is a SharePoint system feature which combines defined metadata and allows SharePoint to locate instances of a content type anywhere on the site by using a content type reference.

For example, you may have a news content type which will define a news piece with a date, title, and the body. This piece of news will also have a layout to structure text boxes and fields gathering the Title and the Date from authors. As you've seen in the earlier scenario, *Publishing Portal*, SharePoint allows users and developers to perform queries on content types and provide pieces of metadata as a result. In practice, we could have a roll-up of the news based on the date for instance, and users would be able to see titles of news releases and a link to the actual news page.

Let's take a look at some more of the branding-specific features and the SharePoint 2013 out-of-the-box UI to manage them:

1. From *http://sp2013/news*, click the **Gear Menu | Site Settings**
2. Under **Web Designer Galleries** click **Masterpages and page layouts**

In this gallery you will find all of the master pages (files with the extension *.**master**) uploaded to the site and page layouts (files with the extension *.**ASPX**). In a typical site scenario, we upload both new master pages and page layouts into one gallery and those can be selected by site administrators and authorized users to be used throughout the site. Let's see how:

1. From the *http://sp2013/news*, click the **Gear Menu | Site Settings**
2. Under the **Look and Feel** click **Masterpage**

Here you have an option to specify the **Site Master Page**, which is the master page which will be used by content pages on the site. The drop-down of options will include more master pages as you upload them, which we'll do later. The **System Master Page** is the master page you see right when you're on the settings page or an item upload page. Since item forms, such as the document upload form or the create new list item form, use a system master page, you may need to customize the **System Master Page** to ensure your forms on the site look appropriate, if you're planning to expose those to users.

The last option on the **Look and Feel** page allows you to set a new **Alternate CSS URL**, which in this case will allow you to inject your own Style Sheet to be used on the site. By specifying your own Style Sheet, you will be able to overwrite the default behavior of the out-of-the-box selectors for a variety of controls, both custom and SharePoint native controls.

Let's take a look at how different the navigation management tool is for publishing sites:

1. Click the **Gear Menu | Site Settings**
2. Click **Navigation**

In here, SharePoint power users are able to define not only the nodes that will appear on the top navigation of the site, but also the underlying pages or sites. They're also able to add their own links and nodes and sort them in one of a few options. By making changes in here, SharePoint saves the settings into the content database and exposes the navigation structure using a specialized navigation object. The default navigation control you see rendered on the site connects to that specialized object and renders HTML based on the data in the object.

Applying branding to the collaboration components

Apart from the navigation being defined right in the navigation tool here, SharePoint also allows you to take the navigation settings from the Managed Metadata store, similarly to how WIKI categories are extracted a few scenarios ago: *Enterprise WIKI | Collaboration essentials | Configuring WIKI categories*. To use managed navigation you would change the default navigation selection from **Structural Navigation** to **Managed Navigation** and picking the term set which holds your navigation.

Since we've looked at how you can change the page layout in earlier scenarios, you can check out the following scenario for more details: *Publishing Portal | How to manage its content*.

Related scenarios

- *Provisioning and applying your own custom page layouts*

3.9 Provisioning and applying your own custom page layouts

Scenario

Now that we know the place and the purpose of the page layout, it's time to take a closer look at what the page layout is all about and how to construct and deploy your own.

Similar to the out-of-the-box master page we looked at earlier, we'll start with exploring one of the out-of-the-box page layouts and see what it's all about.

Set up

Since we'll be using the same set up as we did in the previous scenario, I assume you're all set and ready to go. Otherwise you'll need to create a new Publishing Site instance - check out the earlier scenario: *Publishing Portal | How to create it*. For consistency, in this scenario, I'll assume your publishing site has the URL of: *http://sp2013/news.*

Before we begin

Let's download an existing out-of-the-box page layout:

1. Navigate to the root of your publishing site *http://sp2013/news*

2. Click the **Gear Menu | Site Settings**

3. Under **Wed Designer Galleries** click **Master pages and page layouts**

4. Locate and download the layout called **BlankWebPartPage.aspx**

5. Open the layout in Visual Studio or Notepad++

Before diving into details, let's check out the high level structure of the page layout. Now keep in mind that since the markup of the page layout will render within the markup of the master page, we'll only identify the page layout components and skip the surrounding areas.

Applying branding to the collaboration components

If you remember in our master page overview in the scenario titled: *Working with a SharePoint 2013 master page*, there was a placeholder defined like this:

```
<asp:ContentPlaceHolder id="PlaceHolderMain" runat="server" />
```

Well, this is where the majority of the page layout content will be inserted and it's defined in a page layout within the following section; we'll have a detailed look at this section further here:

```
<asp:Content ContentPlaceHolderId="PlaceHolderMain" runat="server">
<!-- … -->
</asp:Content>
```

For more details on areas within the master page, check out the scenario titled: Working with a SharePoint 2013 master page

If you'd like to explore the same page layout we're looking at, on your publishing portal ensure that the page you're looking at inherits from the Blank Web Part Page layout; to find out how to make this change, check the scenario titled: Publishing Portal | How to manage its content

Figure 3.9.1 Publishing page layout components

Let's take a look at what is involved in a typical page layout structure. Just as before, we'll skip the most obvious or irrelevant pieces. I will comment on areas that you are most likely to work with. Also, to discover more granular pieces of the page layout it's easier and way more efficient to use Firebug or the IE Developer Toolbar.

```
<!--Defines the page layout and inherits functionality from the base
class-->
<%@ Page language="C#"   Inherits="Microsoft.SharePoint.Publishing.
PublishingLayoutPage …


<!-- Contains ASP.NET server controls used on master page and in pages of
the SharePoint site -->
<%@ Register Tagprefix="SharePointWebControls"   …
```

```
<!--Supplies classes and functionality to work with web part pages-->
<%@ Register Tagprefix="WebPartPages" …


<!--Supplies classes and functionality to work with publishing
pages-->
<%@ Register Tagprefix="PublishingWebControls" …


<!-- Contains classes for nodes, data source, providers functionality
implementing SharePoint publishing navigation-->
<%@ Register Tagprefix="PublishingNavigation" Namespace="Microsoft.
SharePoint.Publishing.Navigation" …


<!-- Area dedicated to registering custom CSS and scripts -->
<asp:Content ContentPlaceholderID="PlaceHolderAdditionalPageHead"
runat="server">


<!-- Style sheet providing basic web part page rendering rules-->
<SharePointWebControls:CssRegistration name="<%
$SPUrl:~sitecollection/Style Library/~language/Themable/Core Styles/
pagelayouts15.css %>" runat="server"/>


<!--Anything enclosed in an EditModePanel is only rendered while the
page is in edit mode -->
<PublishingWebControls:EditModePanel runat="server">


<!--The below styles are loaded only when a page is in edit mode-->
<SharePointWebControls:CssRegistration name="<%
$SPUrl:~sitecollection/Style Library/~language/Themable/Core Styles/
editmode15.css %>"
```

```
<!--Truncated section-->
</PublishingWebControls:EditModePanel>
</asp:Content>


<!--Below will be inserted into the PlaceHolderPageTitle part of the
masterpage -->
<!--This will render the page title to the title area in the
browser-->
<asp:Content ContentPlaceHolderId="PlaceHolderPageTitle"
runat="server">
<SharePointWebControls:ListProperty Property="Title" runat="server"/>
- <SharePointWebControls:FieldValue FieldName="Title" runat="server"/>
</asp:Content>


<!--This will be inserted into the PlaceHolderPageTitleInTitleArea
placeholder on your master page … … which is right under the ribbon
and before the rest of the page content goes-->
<asp:Content ContentPlaceHolderId="PlaceHolderPageTitleInTitleArea"
runat="server">
  <SharePointWebControls:FieldValue FieldName="Title" runat="server" />
</asp:Content>


<!--Below is placed inside PlaceHolderTitleBreadcrumb on the master
page, which represents the page breadcrumb-->
<asp:Content ContentPlaceHolderId="PlaceHolderTitleBreadcrumb"
runat="server">

<!-- ... Page breadcrumb control content has been truncated ... -->
</asp:Content>
```

```
<!--The Page description information entered in the page properties
into PlaceHolderPageDescription …
… area on the master page which is right after the title of the page
in this layout -->
<asp:Content ContentPlaceHolderId="PlaceHolderPageDescription"
runat="server">
<SharePointWebControls:ProjectProperty Property="Description"
runat="server"/>
</asp:Content>
```

Now, we're past the header of the page layout as well as some of the control registrations. We've also taken a look at some of the items in the body of the page, such as values from fields on the page being extracted and rendered. Above, when we extract the title and description information, that is an example of how you can extract other pieces of available metadata on the page.

Let's now take a look at the main part of the page where all the content and web part zones are rendered. The main part of the page is something you will be tweaking pretty often to match your scenario.

```
<!--Contents of this area will be placed in the PlaceHolderMain place
holder of the master page designed to render the main content of the
page-->
<asp:Content ContentPlaceHolderId="PlaceHolderMain" runat="server">

<!--A set of controls capturing page metadata; in this case we're
capturing the page title, when the page is saved this information will
be saved along with it -->
<PublishingWebControls:EditModePanel runat="server" CssClass="edit-
mode-panel title-edit">
```

```
<!--If we know the name and the type of other fields the page might
have, such as description, we can add them here and users will be able
to change them right when editing the page -->
<SharePointWebControls:TextField runat="server" FieldName="Title"/>
</PublishingWebControls:EditModePanel>

<!--This is a main content area of the page, you can structure this
area to your liking -->
<div class="welcome-content">

<!--These controls will render the contents of the
PublishingPageContent metadata field on the page which in this case
contains the body of the page-->
<PublishingWebControls:RichHtmlField FieldName="PublishingPageContent"
HasInitialFocus="True" MinimumEditHeight="400px" runat="server"/>

<!--Below the content, this page layout will render web part zones.
Users can add web parts to those …zones while in edit mode. You can
add/remove your web part zones using your own structure -->
<!--This is how a web part zone is declared -->
<WebPartPages:WebPartZone runat="server" Title="Header" ID="Header"/>
</div>

<!--Remaining web part zones were truncated -->
</asp:Content>
```

That's all there is to a page layout. In essence, as you can see, the main part of the content is the structural container for web part zones. The zones, which in the end are going to contain web parts, are placed appropriately on the page surrounded by markup to match your desired look and feel.

The sample we looked at above is quite a complex page layout. In essence, the page

Applying branding to the collaboration components

layout is a simple master page for pages, allowing pages on the same site to have a distinct look.

Let's take a look at how we can provision a page layout using Visual Studio. We'll be using a similar solution to when we provisioned master pages for our collaboration site.

How it's done

1. Open Visual Studio and create a new project using the **SharePoint 2013 Empty Project** template

2. Specify *http://sp2013/news* as your debug URL and choose the **Deploy as a farm solution** option

3. In the solution explorer, locate the **Features** folder and right click on it to add a new feature

4. Rename the default **Feature1** to **ProvisionPageLayout** so we can track our items better. This feature will be used to upload our custom page layout to the gallery

5. In the solution explorer, right click on the project name and select **Add | New Item**....

6. Select **Module** for an item type and give it the name **PageLayouts**

7. Delete the **Sample.txt** file in the module

8. Right click on the module to **Add** and **Existing Item ...**

9. Select the **BlankWebPartPage.aspx** we have downloaded earlier and rename it to **CustomWebPartPage.aspx**

10. Open **Elements.xml** in your **PageLayouts** module in Visual Studio and replace its contents with the following:

```
<?xml version="1.0" encoding="utf-8"?>
<Elements xmlns="http://schemas.microsoft.com/sharepoint/">
```

```
Module Name="PageLayouts" List="116" Url="_catalogs/masterpage">
<File Path="PageLayouts\CustomWebPartPage.aspx"
Type="GhostableInLibrary" Url="CustomWebPartPage.aspx" >
<Property Name="ContentType" Value="$Resources:cmscore,contenttype_
pagelayout_name;" />
</File>
</Module>
</Elements>
```

In here, the Module and File elements are describing where the new page layout is going to be uploaded. The List attribute specifies the master page and page layout gallery URL.

In the File element, the URL defines where the page layout is uploaded. GhostableinLibrary tells SharePoint to create a list item to go with your file when it is added to the library

11. Let's deploy the solution; right click the solution name and click Deploy

12. Wait for the Visual Studio to finish the solution deployment by following the Output windows messages. Navigate back to the site root *http://sp2013/news*

13. Edit the page and ensure you can select a new page from the Page Layouts fly out menu as described in Publishing Portal | How to manage its content

Related scenarios

- *Publishing Portal | How to manage its content*
- *Applying a new SharePoint collaboration site master page*

3.10 Working with search site master page

Scenario

The Search site is one of the integral parts of any collaboration portal so having a consistent look and feel for your search site is important. The Enterprise Search site uses the publishing infrastructure, meaning that it has a master page and page layouts to drive its look. Simple pages such as the default page of the search site have only a search box, which warrants them to use the simplest version of the page layout. The Search results page has a few web part zones to show results, paging controls, refiners, and suggestions, for which more complex page layouts are available. However, all of those page layouts use the same master page and that's where we'll add most of our customizations.

Set up

The Search site should be created and available in your cloudshare environment; however, it's a simple process to create a new instance of one, just follow the steps outline in the earlier scenario: *Enterprise Search Center | How to create it*

Details and Notes

Since most search sites are not complex in their information architecture, they don't have links and menus like the collaboration sites do. To keep our site light and to the point, we'll create a truncated version of the header, just like the one before in the collaboration site example in the scenario: *Applying a custom user interface to a SharePoint collaboration site*. Our end result will look similar to the screenshot below

Chapter 3

Figure 3.10.1 User interface customizations on a search site

How it's done

1. Open Visual Studio and create a new project using the **SharePoint 2013 Empty Project** template

2. Specify *http://sp2013/sites/Search* as your debug URL and choose the **Deploy as a farm solution** option. This assumes your search center has been created with the URL *http://sp2013/sites/Search*, if that's not the case, use the URL of your search center site

3. In the solution explorer, locate the **Features** folder and right click on it to add a new feature

4. Rename the default **Feature1** to **ProvisionSearchMaster** so we can track our items better. This feature will be used to upload our custom master page to the gallery

5. In the solution explorer, right click on the project name and select **Add | New Item**....

6. Select **Module** for an item type and give it the name **Masterpage**

7. Rename the **Sample.txt** file in the module to **searchmaster.master**

8. Click the **Gear Menu | Site Settings | Web Designer Galleries | Master pages and page layouts**

Applying branding to the collaboration components

9. Locate the **seattle.master** and pick **Download a Copy** from the context menu. Save the file to disk

10. Open the newly downloaded master page in Visual Studio and copy its content to the **searchmaster.master** we just created

11. Next, we'll add our custom style sheet to the custom masterpage. Locate the end of the head section in **searchmaster.master**:

    ```
    </head>
    ```
    And add the following code right before the `</head>`

    ```
    <link rel="stylesheet" type="text/css" href="/_layouts/15/
    CustomSearchSite/style.css" />
    ```

12. Next let's create the style sheet; right click the Visual Studio project name you created and select **Add** | **SharePoint "Layouts" Mapped Folder**

13. Rename the folder created underneath the **Layouts** folder to **CustomSearchSite**

14. Right click on the **CustomSearchSite** | select **Add** | **New Item** | select **Web** category | select **Style Sheet** as a project item | name the file **style.css**

15. Add the following CSS into the **style.css**, check out the inline comments for details

    ```
    /**NOTE - The #suiteBar is broken into two sections,
    #suiteBarLeft(first section), #suiteBarRight(second section) **/


    /**Removing the out out-of-the-box height, added custom background**/
    #suiteBar{
          height: 38px;
          background: url("/_layouts/15/images/CustomSearchSite/suitebar-
    BG3.png") repeat-x;}


    /**Start of left Suitebar**/
    ```

```css
/**Removed the out-of-the-box light blue color**/
#suiteBar #suiteBarLeft{
     background-color: transparent;}


/**Placed the custom background under the SharePoint title section**/
#suiteBar #suiteBarLeft .LeftSuiteBG{background: url("/_layouts/15/images/CustomSearchSite/suitebar-BG1.png") repeat-x;}


/** The final piece to our background, placed to the far right**/
#suiteBar #suiteBarLeft .LeftSuiteBG .InnerSuitBarContainer {
     height: 38px;
/**NOTE - No need to float:left, we took advantage of the divs width and used 100% on the backgroun image**/
background: url("/_layouts/15/images/CustomSearchSite/suitbar-BG2.png") no-repeat 100% 0;}


/**Padding is used to horizontally align the title, changed the out-of-the-box white color, made the title bold**/
#suiteBar #suiteBarLeft .LeftSuiteBG .InnerSuiteBarContainer .ms-core-brandingText{
     color:#0D7C0D;
     font-weight: 600;
     padding-top: 8px;}


/**Added the padding to horizontally align the Newsfeed, SkyDrive, sites links**/
#suiteBar #suiteBarLeft .ms-core-suiteLinkList .ms-core-suiteLink span{padding-top:8px;}
```

Applying branding to the collaboration components

```css
/**Adjusting the hover over the background height for the Newsfeed,
SkyDrive, sites links**/
.ms-core-suiteLink-a, .ms-core-suiteLink-a:visited, a.ms-core-
suiteLink-disabled{height:33px;}

/**Start of Suitebar right**/
/**Removing the white hover over from the administrator link**/
#suiteBar #suiteBarRight .ms-welcome-hover, .ms-siteactions-hover{
border-radius: 10px;
background-color:#96bf96;
border-right-color: transparent;}
```

16. As you see, our CSS is using few custom images, let's add those to our Visual Studio solution; right click the Visual Studio project name you created and select **Add | SharePoint "Images" Mapped Folder**

17. Rename the folder created underneath the **Images** folder to **CustomSearchSite**

18. Right click on the **CustomSearchSite** | select **Add** | **Existing Item** | select the following files from the package provided with this scenario:

    a. **suitebar-BG1.png** – left slice of the custom suite bar image
    b. **suitebar-BG2.png** – middle slice of the custom suite bar image
    c. **suitebar-BG3.png** – right slice of the custom suite bar image

19. To ensure our images are able to hang on to the suite bar, we'll add a few selectors to the out-of-the-box markup of our master page; locate the following section in our master page:

```
<div class="ms-tableCell ms-verticalAlignMiddle
```

Add class named **LeftSuiteBG** to the list of existing classes so the section looks like this:

```
<div class="ms-tableCell ms-verticalAlignMiddle LeftSuiteBG">
```

Locate the following control right below the section:

```
<SharePoint:DelegateControl id="ID_SuiteBarBrandingDelegate" Control
Id="SuiteBarBrandingDelegate" runat="server" />
```

And wrap it with another DIV as shown below:

```
<div class="InnerSuiteBarContainer">
<SharePoint:DelegateControl id="ID_SuiteBarBrandingDelegate" Control
Id="SuiteBarBrandingDelegate" runat="server" />
</div>
```

20. Open **Elements.xml** in your master page module in Visual Studio and replace its contents with the following master page provisioning code:

```
<?xml version="1.0" encoding="utf-8"?>
<Elements xmlns="http://schemas.microsoft.com/sharepoint/">
<Module Name="MasterPage" List="116" Url="_catalogs/masterpage">
<File Path="MasterPage\searchmaster.master" Type="GhostableInLibrary"
Url="searchmaster.master" />
</Module>
</Elements>
```

21. Now that our solution takes care of deploying the master page, let's add the code to set the master page as a current on the site, otherwise SharePoint will keep using **seattle.master**.
    Locate the **Features** folder in your solution and right click on **ProvisionSearchMaster** in it. Select, **Add Event Receiver**

22. In the **FeatureActivated** section of the code, replace the commented section with

the following code:

```
public override void FeatureActivated(SPFeatureReceiverProperties properties)
{
  SPWeb web = properties.Feature.Parent as SPWeb;
  web.CustomMasterUrl = "/_catalogs/masterpage/searchmaster.master";
  web.MasterUrl = "/_catalogs/masterpage/searchmaster.master";
  web.Update();
  web.Dispose();
}
```

23. Let's deploy the solution; right click the solution name and click **Deploy**

Wait for Visual Studio to finish the solution deployment by following the **Output** windows messages. Navigate back to the site root of our search site *http://sp2013/sites/Search/Pages/default.aspx* to check out our latest customization to the look and feel of the page, which should look similar to below

Figure 3.10.2 Branded search site

3.11 The basics: Changing the look and feel of Personal Site

Scenario

A SharePoint Personal Site represents a special type of site reserved for users to hold their personal work related information, as well as to interact with other users. Due to the nature of the Personal Site technical design, making user interface customizations is somewhat different. In this scenario well take a look at how you can apply your own branding to the Personal Sites of all users to match your corporate site look and feel.

Set up

Provided you're using a CloudShare SharePoint 2013 development environment, you will have SharePoint Personal Sites set up and available. Typically SharePoint Personal sites reside on a separate SharePoint web application, in our case the URL is: *http://sp2013:8080*.

To learn how you can set up personal sites on your environment refer to an earlier scenario in chapter 2 *Personal Site | How to create it*.

As mentioned earlier, a personal site will consist of two parts:

1. A general profile area with page content which will change depending on the logged in user. This area is usually the root of your Personal Sites web application, in our case *http://sp2013:8080*. This area is shared among all users and changes applied here will be visible to everyone.

2. A user's Personal Site with personal document libraries and lists. This area is individual for each user who has a personal site and changes applied here will be only visible to this user.

Before we begin

At first it's transparent from the user interface standpoint for users to switch between the general profile area and the actual personal site. After all, there is no **Site Settings** link available to an administrator where they can edit the page.

Applying branding to the collaboration components

To access the settings of the general profile area navigate to: *http://sp2013:8080/_layouts/15/settings.aspx*

To access the personal site for an administrator follow the URL convention similar to this: *http://sp2013srv:8080/personal/administrator/_layouts/15/settings.aspx*

You can change the look of both areas just as if you were to change it in a team site. Even though, the link to the design gallery is not available in the **Settings** menu, you can access it using the following relative *URL: /_layouts/15/designgallery.aspx*.

You might assume that since the look and feel editing experience is just like in a team site, customizing the personal site is just as you would customize it for the team site, and you're right. A Personal Site has a bit different layout as you can tell, the header is smaller and the main content area is larger.

This is facilitated by the default personal site master page called **mysite15.master**. You can locate this master page from the settings page */_layouts/15/settings.aspx* | under **Web Designer Galleries** | click **Mater pages**.

To get started with customizing the personal site means you need to get started with the out-of-the-box **mysite15.master**

Let's take a brief walk through the **mysite15.master** and since it's so similar to its relative **seattle.master**, we will only go over the main areas, since there are more interesting parts of the personal site customization in front of us.

1. Download a new version of **mysite15.master** from */_layouts/15/settings.aspx* | under **Web Designer Galleries** | click **Master pages**

2. Open the **mysite15.master** in Visual Studio or Notepad++ and let's go over the main sections below

We'll skip the control registration and the header since it's nearly identical in both master pages.

The first block of interest in this code is the section below in the main area of the master page

```
<div id="s4-workspace" class="ms-core-overlay">
```
The first difference is that the area dedicated to the site icon doesn't exist in **mysite15.master**, which makes sense since the site icon will be replaced by the user's photo.

```
<div id="siteIcon" class="ms-tableCell ms-verticalAlignTop">
<!-- This area doesn't exist in mysite15.master -->
</div>
```

Next, the breadcrumb section doesn't exist in **mysite15.master**, which is also reasonable since personal sites will have a prescribed user interface and users will not be able to manage their own breadcrumb out-of-the-box.

```
<div class="ms-breadcrumb-dropdownBox">
<!-- This area doesn't exist in mysite15.master -->
</div>
```

The top navigation is also absent from the **mysite15.master** due to the prescribed structure of personal sites:

```
<SharePoint:AjaxDelta id="DeltaTopNavigation" BlockElement="true"
CssClass="ms-displayInline ms-core-navigation" role="navigation"
runat="server">
<!-- This area doesn't exist in mysite15.master -->
</SharePoint:AjaxDelta>
```

The page title and description are also not present, to minimize the header and maximize the content area:

```
<h1 id="pageTitle" class="ms-core-pageTitle">
<!-- This area doesn't exist in mysite15.master -->
</h1>
```

The search area is slightly lower in the page hierarchy and it's not in the header as it is for team sites:

Applying branding to the collaboration components

```
<asp:ContentPlaceHolder id="PlaceHolderSearchArea" runat="server">
<!-- This area is slightly rearranged and moved down in mysite15.
master -->
</asp:ContentPlaceHolder>
```

Moving through the markup of the **mysite15.master** we see that next significant area in the list is:

```
<div id="sideNavBox" class="ms-dialogHidden ms-forceWrap ms-noList ms-mysite-sideNavBox">
```

This section contains the left navigation and any elements that sit in the left section of the page, such as a user's photo, which is the first on the list:

```
<SharePoint:AjaxDelta id="DeltaPlaceHolderProfileImage"
BlockElement="true" runat="server"> <SPSWC:ProfilePropertyImage
CssClass="ms-profile-image" name="onetidHeadbnnr0" ID="PictureUrlImage"
ShowPlaceholder="TRUE"
RenderProfileLinks="TRUE"
PropertyName="PictureUrl"
ImageSize="2" runat="server"/>
</SharePoint:AjaxDelta>
```

If the user hasn't uploaded a photo, a placeholder image is displayed.

The next item present in **mysite15.master**, and not in **seattle.master** is the **user quick launch**; this is a special quick launch, which instead of displaying document libraries, like it does on a team site, displays: Newsfeed, About Me, and Site Contents. You can add more links for all users by navigating to *_layouts/15/settings.aspx* | **Look and Feel** | **Quick Launch** | add any desired links using the interface here.

```
<div id="js-mysite-userquicklaunch" style="display: none; ">
<SharePoint:DelegateControl runat="server"
```

```
ControlId="MySiteUserQLDataSource">
<!--Truncated section -->
</Template_Controls>
</SharePoint:DelegateControl>
</div>
```

Those are the main differences worth mentioning related to design of the personal site.

Next, let's take a look at how we can deploy a custom master page to the personal site for all users. Remember that changes applied on this site will show on the newsfeed and profile pages for all users and not just for an individual user personal site.

How it's done

1. Open Visual Studio and create a new project using **SharePoint 2013 Empty Project** template

2. Specify *http://sp2013:8080* as your debug URL and choose **Deploy as a farm solution** option

3. In the solution explorer, locate the **Features** folder and right click on it to add a new feature

4. Rename the default **Feature1** to **ProvisionPersonalMaster** so we can track our items better. This feature will be used to upload our custom master page to the gallery

5. In the solution explorer, right click on the project name and select **Add | New Item**....

6. Select **Module** for an item type and give it the name **Masterpage**

7. Rename the **Sample.txt** file in the module to **newmaster.master**

8. Navigate to *http://sp2013/_layouts/15/settings.aspx* logged in as administrator

9. Click the **Gear Menu | Site Settings** and locate **Masterpages** under **Web Designer Galleries**.

Applying branding to the collaboration components

10. Locate the **mysite15.master** and pick **Download a Copy** from the context menu. Save the file to disk.

11. Open the newly downloaded master page in Visual Studio and copy its content to the **newmaster.master** we just created

12. Locate the end of the head section in **newmaster.master**:

    ```
    </head>
    ```
    And add the following code right before the `</head>`

    ```html
    <link rel="stylesheet" type="text/css" href="/_layouts/15/CustomPersonalSites/style.css" />
    ```

13. Next let's create the style sheet; right click the Visual Studio project name you created and select **Add | SharePoint "Layouts" Mapped Folder**

14. Rename the folder created underneath the **Layouts** folder to **CustomPersonalSites**

15. Right click on the **CustomPersonalSites** | select **Add** | **New Item** | select **Web** category | select **Style Sheet** as a project item | name the file **style.css**

16. Add the following CSS into the **style.css**, check out the inline comments for details

    ```css
    /**NOTE - The #suiteBar is broken into two sections,
    #suiteBarLeft(first section), #suiteBarRight(second section) **/

    /**Removing the out out-of-the-box height, added a custom
    background**/
    #suiteBar{
         height: 38px;
         background: url("/_layouts/15/images/CustomPersonalSites/suitebar-BG3.png") repeat-x;}

    /**Start of left Suitebar**/
    ```

```css
/**Removed the out-of-the-box light blue color**/
#suiteBar #suiteBarLeft{
      background-color: transparent;}


/**Placed the custom background under the SharePoint title section**/
#suiteBar #suiteBarLeft .LeftSuiteBG{background: url("/_layouts/15/
images/CustomPersonalSites/suitebar-BG1.png") repeat-x;}


/**The final piece to our background, placed to the far right**/
#suiteBar #suiteBarLeft .LeftSuiteBG .InnerSuiteBarContainer {
      height: 38px;
/**NOTE - No need to float:left, we took advantage of the divs width
and used 100% on the backgroun image**/
background: url("/_layouts/15/images/CustomPersonalSites/suitebar-
BG2.png") no-repeat 100% 0;}


/**Padding used to horizontally align the title, changed the out-of-
the-box white color, made the title bold**/
#suiteBar #suiteBarLeft .LeftSuiteBG .InnerSuiteBarContainer .ms-
core-brandingText{
      color:#0D7C0D;
      font-weight: 600;
      padding-top: 8px;}


/**Added padding to horizontally align the Newsfeed, SkyDrive, sites
links**/
#suiteBar #suiteBarLeft .ms-core-suiteLinkList .ms-core-suiteLink
span{padding-top:8px;}
```

Applying branding to the collaboration components

```
/**Adjusting hover over background height for the Newsfeed, SkyDrive,
sites links**/
.ms-core-suiteLink-a, .ms-core-suiteLink-a:visited, a.ms-core-
suiteLink-disabled{height:33px;}

/**Start of Suitbar right**/
/**Removing the white hover over from the administrator link**/
#suiteBar #suiteBarRight .ms-welcome-hover, .ms-siteactions-hover{
border-radius: 10px;
background-color:#96bf96;
border-right-color: transparent;}
```

17. You'll notice our CSS is using a few custom images, let's add those to our Visual Studio solution; right click the Visual Studio project name you created and select **Add | SharePoint "Images" Mapped Folder**

18. Rename the folder created underneath the **Images** folder to **CustomPersonalSites**

19. Right click on the **CustomPersonalSites** | select **Add** | **Existing Item** | select the following files from the package provided with this scenario:

    a. **suitebar-BG1.png** – left slice of the custom suite bar image
    b. **suitebar-BG2.png** – middle slice of the custom suite bar image
    c. **suitebar-BG3.png** – right slice of the custom suite bar image

20. To ensure our images are able to hang on to the suite bar, we'll add a few selectors to out-of-the-box markup of our master page; locate the following section in our masterpage:

```
<div class="ms-tableCell ms-verticalAlignMiddle
```

Add a class named **LeftSuiteBG** to the list of existing classes so the section looks like this:

```
<div class="ms-tableCell ms-verticalAlignMiddle LeftSuiteBG">
```

Locate the following control right below the section:

```
<SharePoint:DelegateControl id="ID_SuiteBarBrandingDelegate" Control
Id="SuiteBarBrandingDelegate" runat="server" />
```

And wrap it with another DIV as shown below:

```
<div class="InnerSuiteBarContainer">
<SharePoint:DelegateControl id="ID_SuiteBarBrandingDelegate" Control
Id="SuiteBarBrandingDelegate" runat="server" />
</div>
```

21. Open **Elements.xml** in your master page module in Visual Studio and replace its contents with the following master page provisioning code:

```
<?xml version="1.0" encoding="utf-8"?>
<Elements xmlns="http://schemas.microsoft.com/sharepoint/">
  <Module Name="MasterPage" List="116" Url="_catalogs/masterpage">
      <File Path="MasterPage\newmaster.master"
Type="GhostableInLibrary" Url="newmaster.master" />
  </Module>
</Elements>
```

22. Now that our solution takes care of deploying the master page, let's add the code to set the master page as current on the site, otherwise SharePoint will keep using **mysite15.master**.

    Locate the **Features** folder in your solution and right click on **ProvisionPersonalMaster** in it. Select, **Add Event Receiver**

23. In the **FeatureActivated** section of the code, replace the commented section with

Applying branding to the collaboration components

the following code:

```
public override void FeatureActivated(SPFeatureReceiverProperties
properties)
{
   SPWeb web = properties.Feature.Parent as SPWeb;
   web.CustomMasterUrl = "/_catalogs/masterpage/newmaster.master";
   web.MasterUrl = "/_catalogs/masterpage/newmaster.master";
   web.Update();
   web.Dispose();
}
```

24. Let's deploy the solution; right click the solution name and click **Deploy**

Wait for Visual Studio to finish the solution deployment by following the **Output** windows messages. Navigate back to the site root *http://sp2013:8080* to check out our latest customization to the look and feel of the page which should look similar to below

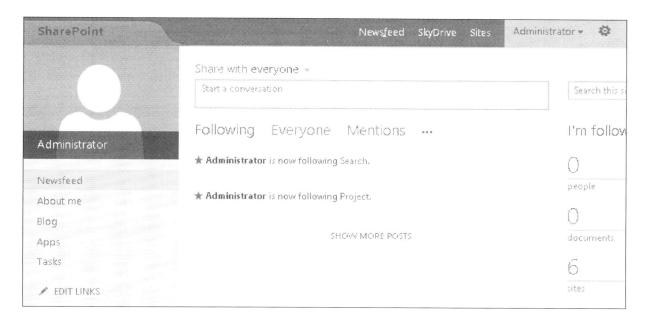

Figure 3.11.1 Branded personal site

Related scenarios

- *Applying a custom user interface to a SharePoint collaboration site*
- *Changing the look and feel of Personal Sites for individual users*

3.12 Changing the look and feel of Personal Sites for individual users

Scenario

As discussed in the previous scenario, Personal Sites consist of two parts. The first part, as fully discussed in the previous scenario, hosts general pages, such as newsfeed and profile pages, for all users. When you apply your custom branding to those pages, everyone will see the new look and feel. However, when users click SkyDrive for example, they are taken to their own instance of a Personal Site. If you'd like to have your overall site look consistently, you need to apply branding for individual Personal Sites. This can be quite tedious because you can have quite a few sites already created for a variety of users. In this scenario, we'll build on the top of the existing customization discussed in the previous scenario, and learn how we can create an automated deployment script to deploy our branding to multiple sites.

Set up

For continuity, we'll use exactly the same set up as in the previous scenario; some parts of our Visual Studio solution will also be reused.

We'll also be using a PowerShell script which will help us deploy our custom master page to a number of Personal Sites.

Download and extract the source accompanying this scenario: *SetupPersonalSiteBranding*. In the package provided you will find 3 files, copy those into the same directory in your development environment:

- **SetupPersonalSiteBranding.ps1** – script for performing installation of our custom branding onto a set of personal sites
- **StartScript.bat** – starting point for the script
- **Config.xml** – configuration file defining which sites will receive our custom branding

How it's done

1. Assuming you have already deployed our custom master page for the personal site created in scenario: *The basics: Changing the look and feel of Personal Site*, open the Visual Studio solution we have created in the last scenario.

2. In the solution explorer, locate the **Features** folder and double click on the feature provisioning the master page, called **ProvisionPersonalMaster**

3. Click the **Manifest** tab at the top of the **Features** page; you will be switched to the XML view with various properties we have assigned using the UI

Figure 3.12.1 Visual Studio feature manifest

4. Locate the attribute called **Id** of the **Feature** element and copy the value of it, which is going to look something like this: 04da9931-a167-4e30-be8a-905b5348e3bf. We will be referencing this further on in our configuration file

5. Now, using Notepad++ or Visual Studio, open the **Config.xml** you have copied from the source code package, you will see a listing similar to below:

```
<?xml version="1.0" encoding="utf-8"?>

<Setup WebAppUrl="http://sp2013:8080">
```

Applying branding to the collaboration components

```xml
<SiteCollections>
<SiteCollection Url="/administrator" ManagedPath="/personal">
<Features>
<Feature Id="04da9931-a167-4e30-be8a-905b5348e3bf"
Name="SharePointProject1_ProvisionPersonalMaster"></Feature>
</Features>
</SiteCollection>
</SiteCollections>
</Setup>
```

6. Modify the value in the file as below:

    a. **WebAppUrl** – set to the URL of your SharePoint web application

    b. **SiteCollection** – is a node representing each individual user site we'll be branding, for now we have just one individual personal site

    c. **SiteCollection** node | **Url** attribute – the URL of the individual user site; in our case, it's an individual site for the **administrator** user

    d. **SiteCollection** node | **ManagedPath** attribute – the **Managed Path** for all individual user sites defined in Central Administration; this value is usually set to *personal* by default

    e. **Feature** node | **Id** attribute – replace the value of the **Id** to the Feature Id you have copied in step 4

    f. **Feature** node | **Name** attribute – replace the name to the concatenated value of your Visual Studio project name and the Feature which provisions the master page: **[ProjectName]_[MasterPageFeatureName]**; in our case it's **SharePointProject1_ProvisionPersonalMaster**

7. If you have more than one user site you'd like to apply the custom master page to, you simply need to copy the **<SiteCollection>** node and change the value for the user name leaving all the other parameters the same. For example, below is how our configuration script would look like for 2 users: **administrator** and **user1**

```xml
<?xml version="1.0" encoding="utf-8"?>
```

```xml
<Setup WebAppUrl="http://sp2013:8080">
<SiteCollections>
<SiteCollection Url="/administrator" ManagedPath="/personal">
<Features>
<Feature Id="04da9931-a167-4e30-be8a-905b5348e3bf"
Name="SharePointProject1_ProvisionPersonalMaster"></Feature>
</Features>
</SiteCollection>
<SiteCollection Url="/user1" ManagedPath="/personal">
<Features>
<Feature Id="04da9931-a167-4e30-be8a-905b5348e3bf"
Name="SharePointProject1_ProvisionPersonalMaster"></Feature>
</Features>
</SiteCollection>
</SiteCollections>
</Setup>
```

8. Save the **Config.xml** file and launch the script by clicking on the **StartScript.bat**

Note: If you're receiving an error in the script output about SharePoint not being able to find the feature SharePointProject1_ProvisionPersonalMaster, ensure you have deployed the Visual Studio solution from the previous scenario; later we'll take a look at how to automate this process without having Visual Studio installed on your environment.

To verify the customization you need to log into the main portal with the credentials of another user. Then navigate to the individual personal site by clicking SkyDrive. The individual personal sites will be created for the users with the custom look and feel applied.

Related scenarios

- *Applying a custom user interface to a SharePoint collaboration site*
- *Changing the look and feel of Personal Sites for individual users*

3.13 Putting it all together: automated installation of your branding package to multiple environments

Scenario

So far we've looked at how you can build custom branding for a variety of types of templates. We used Visual Studio to deploy our customizations one by one, which was relatively simple. Now, think about deploying the entire set of customizations. After all, you probably want to deploy your core site customizations, sub sites, search, and personal sites all in one. Especially if your company uses a staging and production environment, you now have to do the same for all of those environments and no administrator will install Visual Studio on the production environment. That's why, in this scenario, we'll learn how to take your branding customizations and install them all as one automated installation package. We've looked at what a SharePoint Solution Package is all about in the scenario *Setting up and understanding your development environment*, now let's install it using an automated script.

Set up

This scenario assumes you have gone through building all of the branding packages and either have them ready, or at least your environment is configured so that you have at least the following instances of the site templates:

1. Publishing Site instance: *http://sp2013/sites/news*
2. Team Site instance: *http://sp2013/sites/team*
3. WIKI Site instance: *http://sp2013/sites/wiki*
4. Enterprise Search Site instance: *http://sp2013/sites/search*

We'll be using PowerShell for our script just like we did in the scenario entitled: *Changing the look and feel of Personal Sites for individual users*

Before we begin

As mentioned just above, we're going to be using a PowerShell script to install our

Applying branding to the collaboration components

customizations. As much as PowerShell is a powerful and exciting framework and tool, we won't be digging into the details of the script. PowerShell for SharePoint is a topic for an entire book and in fact I have written one along with many other great authors. Having said that, if PowerShell automation in this scenario fascinates you, feel free to check out the source code of the script available for this scenario and take a read through the comments which explain the execution flow.

Also check out the *Related Scenarios* section of this scenario to see what other PowerShell automation scripts we're going to use in this book.

How it's done

1. Download and extract the source code accompanying this scenario. The source code represents a PowerShell script used to deploy our entire customization

2. Open the **Config.xml** from the package using Visual Studio or Notepad++. The resulting configuration file should look similar to below:

```xml
<?xml version="1.0" encoding="utf-8"?>

<Setup WebAppUrl="http://sp2013srv">
<Solutions>
<Solution WebApplication="False">Project.Branding.wsp</Solution>
</Solutions>

<SiteCollections>
<SiteCollection Url="/news" ManagedPath="/Sites">
<Features>
    <Feature Name="SharePointProject1_ ProvisionPageLayout " Id="04da9931-a167-4e30-be8a-905b5348e3bf"/>
</Features>
</SiteCollection>
<SiteCollection Url="/team" ManagedPath="/Sites">
```

```
<Features>
        <Feature Name="SharePointProject1_ProvisionCollabMaster"
Id="04da9931-a167-4e30-be8a-905b5348e3bf"/>
</Features>
</SiteCollection>
<SiteCollection Url="/wiki" ManagedPath="/Sites">
<Features>
        <Feature Name="SharePointProject1_ProvisionCollabMaster"
Id="04da9931-a167-4e30-be8a-905b5348e3bf"/>
</Features>
</SiteCollection>
<SiteCollection Url="/search" ManagedPath="/Sites">
<Features>
        <Feature Name="SharePointProject1_ ProvisionCollabMaster "
Id="04da9931-a167-4e30-be8a-905b5348e3bf"/>
</Features>
</SiteCollection>
</SiteCollections>

</Setup>
```

3. Ensure the following values reflect your environment:

    a. **WebAppUrl** – set to the URL of your SharePoint web application

    b. **SiteCollections** – is a set of nodes representing each individual site we'll be applying branding to

    c. **SiteCollection** node | **Url** attribute – the URLs of the sites

    d. **SiteCollection** node | **ManagedPath** attribute – the **Managed Path** for each site; in our case it's the default **sites**

Applying branding to the collaboration components

    e. **Feature** node | **Id** attribute – the value of the specific **Id** for the Feature responsible for the master page provisioning. This feature **Id** will be different for some sites

    f. **Feature** node | **Name** attribute – replace the name to the concatenated value of your Visual Studio project name and the Feature which provisions the master page: **[ProjectName]_[MasterPageFeatureName]**; in our case it's going to be similar to **SharePointProject1_ProvisionCollabMaster**

4. Open the Visual Studio solution referenced in the scenario: *Provisioning and applying your own custom page layouts*. This solution package will give us a custom page layout for our **/news** site

5. Create a SharePoint Solution Package by right clicking the **project name** in solution explorer | select **Rebuild**

6. Right click on the **project name** again | select **Open Folder in Windows Explorer** | navigate to **Bin/Debug** | copy the solution package file (*.WSP) to the same directory as our PowerShell script. Rename the solution package to: **PublishingBranding.WSP**

7. In the Visual Studio solution, open the **ProvisionPageLayout** feature and retrieve it's **Id** by using the **Manifest** tab as we did before.

8. Add the **Id** to the **Config.xml** node responsible for the deployment of our **/news** site

    ```
    <Feature Name="[Your project name]_ ProvisionPageLayout " Id="[Your feature Id]"/>
    ```

    Ensure the name of the feature is also in the format **[ProjectName]_[FeatureName]**

9. Open the Visual Studio solution referenced in the scenario: *Applying new SharePoint collaboration site master page*. This solution package will give us a custom page layout for our **/team** and **/wiki** sites

10. Repeat steps 5-8, this time for the feature name use **ProvisionCollabMaster** for both **/team** and **/wiki** sites in our **Config.xml** file. Rename the resulting solution package to: **CollabBranding.WSP**

11. Open the Visual Studio solution referenced in the scenario: *Working with search site master page*. This solution package will give us a custom page layout for our **/search** site

12. Repeat steps 5-8, this time for the feature name use **ProvisionSearchMaster** for the **/search** site in our **Config.xml** file. Rename the resulting solution package to: **SearchBranding.WSP**

13. Add the collected 3 WSP file names to the **<Solutions>** section of your **Config.xml** file which should give you the following result:

    ```
    <Solutions>
    <Solution WebApplication="False"> PublishingBranding.WSP </Solution>
    <Solution WebApplication="False"> CollabBranding.WSP </Solution>
    <Solution WebApplication="False"> SearchBranding.WSP </Solution>
    </Solutions>
    ```

14. Now that the script and all of the related solutions are ready, you can execute the script and confirm that the configurations have been applied to the site.

Related scenarios

- *Automating SharePoint site provisioning and configuration*
- *Provisioning content pages to your site*
- *Provisioning web parts, views and other content to your pages*

CHAPTER 4

Customizing features of your collaboration solution

In this chapter:

- Extending collaboration site templates
- Extending publishing and other site templates
- Provisioning content pages to your site
- Provisioning web parts, views and other content to your pages
- Creating SharePoint lists and performing content roll up
- Capturing list events and executing custom logic on events triggering
- Debugging your SharePoint solution
- Customizing SharePoint structured and managed navigation
- Customizing SharePoint 2013 suite bar menu
- Working with user profiles and user profile properties
- Creating custom user profile properties
- Using user profile property values in your solution
- Creating recurring background running processes using SharePoint timer jobs
- Defining content expiration and automating provisioning of out-of-the-box workflows
- Getting started with building SharePoint 2013 apps

Customizing features of your collaboration solution

4.1 Extending collaboration site templates

Scenario

As we have seen, site templates drive the look and functionality of the site. In the last several scenarios we've learned how you can customize the look and feel of existing site instances. In this scenario we'll take a look at how to create your own template with those customizations already included.

Whether your organization uses a team site, a community site, or several project sites, one thing in common for all of these site instances is they derive from a collaboration site template. In this scenario, we`ll take a look at what are some of the basic building blocks go in to the collaboration site template and how you can extend those building blocks.

Set up

I'm assuming you have an existing instance of the Team Site you created earlier. You will also require Visual Studio 2012 installed in your development environment. If you're using pre-created SharePoint 2013 development environment from CloudShare, then you are ready to go. For more information on how to get Visual Studio 2012 on your environment, search for *Installing Visual Studio MSDN*.

Before we begin

To illustrate site templates schematically we first need to understand that just as there are sites and webs, there are also site templates and web templates. The difference is straightforward: site templates are used to create instances of site collections and web templates define webs.
Let's take a look at the diagram below to see what site templates are made of:

Chapter 4

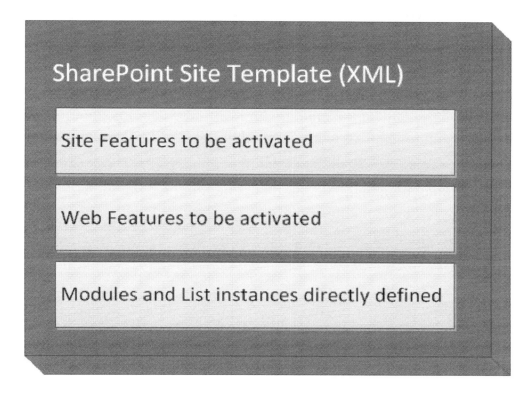

Figure 4.1.1 SharePoint site template structure

As we'll see further, a site template is just an XML file, much like the master page module we provisioned earlier. This XML file is built in a way that its content is understood by SharePoint as a site or web template. As such it appears in the SharePoint user interface when users attempt to create a new site/web. Site templates typically do not directly provision any modules or files, they're just XML definitions. As we'll see next, site templates have 2 major reference sections: site features and web features. Web templates naturally have only reference to web features.

The features referenced by a site or web template must be installed by your custom solution, be pre-installed, or available out-of-the-box.

The mechanics of creating a new site template are simple: when a user creates an instance of a site or web, SharePoint creates a site or web record in its database and attempts to activate features referenced in the template.

When a site or a web is created, it's entire functionality and look is built off the features that

Customizing features of your collaboration solution

the template references. For example, if you forget to reference a feature which provisions a custom home page to a site, your site will exist and there might be document libraries in it, but users will not be able to access them from the home page and receive a *404 Page Not Found Error* instead.

The most logical way to create a custom site template is to pick one of the out-of-the-box site templates which most closely satisfy your needs and use that template as a base. We'll do exactly that in a next section.

How it's done

1. Create a new Visual Studio project: **File | New | Project** and pick a template **Templates | Visual C# | Office/SharePoint | SharePoint Solutions | SharePoint 2013 Empty Project**

2. Specify *http://sp2013* as your debug URL and choose **Deploy as a farm solution** option

3. In the solution explorer, right click on the project name and select **Add | New Item....** | select **Site Definition** project item

4. Set **CustomTeamSite** as the name for your **Site Definition**

5. Expand the newly created **CustomTeamSite** project item folder within Visual Studio and open the file called **webtemp_CustomTeamSite.xml**. This file describes the template such as title, description, etc; its special naming convention makes an association between an actual template and the template description.

6. The **<Configuration>** node within the template description will actually describe the site template.

```
<Configuration ID="0" Title="CustomTeamSite" Hidden="FALSE"
ImageUrl="/_layouts/images/CPVW.gif" Description="CustomTeamSite"
DisplayCategory="SharePoint Customizations">
    </Configuration>
```

Here are some of the values from the template you might want to change:

a. **Title** – title of the template as it appears for users when they create it

b. **Hidden** – sometimes you don't want users to see the template in SharePoint interface and only allow creation of the template using an automated script. One of the ways to achieve that is by making the template hidden

c. **ImageUrl** – the URL of the image to preview the template; it must be accessible within the farm, so it's best placed in a mapped folder

d. **Description** – description of the template

e. **DisplayCategory** – is the category in SharePoint interface where users can locate your template

Here is how they're going to be displayed once the template is deployed. Note: since this is a site template, below is the a snapshot of templates available in Central Administration

Figure 4.1.2 Site template selection user interface

7. In the expanded **CustomTeamSite** project item folder within Visual Studio open the file called **onet.xml**. This file is where the template references all the features. Its code

Customizing features of your collaboration solution

will be similar to below:

```xml
<Configuration ID="0" Name="CustomTeamSite">
     <Lists/>
     <SiteFeatures>
     </SiteFeatures>
     <WebFeatures>
     </WebFeatures>
     <Modules>
       <Module Name="DefaultBlank" />
     </Modules>
</Configuration>
```

In here, we've got sections for our **<SiteFeatures>**, **<WebFeatures>**, and directly declared modules **<Modules>**. In our case, the only module available is the one provisioning the landing page for the provisioned site. We can certainly have as many modules deployed as we want as part of Web or Site features

8. Let's take a look at the out-of-the-box version of a team site template definition by opening the following path from the server file system:
C:\Program Files\Common Files\microsoft shared\Web Server Extensions\15\TEMPLATE\SiteTemplates

9. Locate and open the folder named **sts**, which stands for SharePoint Team Site. In it, open the file **XML\ONET.xml**; for readability, open the file in Visual Studio or Notepad++

10. Locate below section in the file :

```xml
<Configuration ID="0" Name="Default" MasterUrl="_catalogs/masterpage/seattle.master">
```

This is a configuration of the template available to users when they create new team site from Central Administration

11. Copy the **MasterUrl** attribute and it's value to the **onet.xml** in our Visual Studio solution since we'd like to use SharePoint out-of-the-box master page for our custom team site

12. In the out-of-the-box SharePoint Team Site **ONET.xml** on the file system, copy the nodes, including content, of both **<SiteFeatures>** and **<WebFeatures>** and paste it into the respective areas in our own Visual Studio solution. Features here activate basic Team Site functionality such as out-of-the-box lists and web parts.

13. We won't be copying the default landing page of the out-of-the-box team site residing in the **<Module>** since we already have our own. We're also not going to create an instance of the list available in the out-of-the-box site template declared in this section **<Lists>…</Lists>**. We can always provision any out-of-the-box or custom list instances using features, which we're planning to do

14. Let's deploy the solution; right click the solution name and click **Deploy**

15. Wait for the Visual Studio to finish the solution deployment by following the **Output** windows messages. Navigate back to the **Central Administration** site | under **Application Management** | click **Create site collections**.

16. Fill in the details below:

    a. **Title** – CustomTeamSite
    b. **Url** - CustomTS
    c. **Template Selection** – **SharePoint Customizations** category | **CustomTeamSite**
    d. **Primary Site Collection Administrator** – administrator

17. Click **OK**

Once the site has been provisioned, navigate to the URL provided and you will see a site similar to below:

Customizing features of your collaboration solution

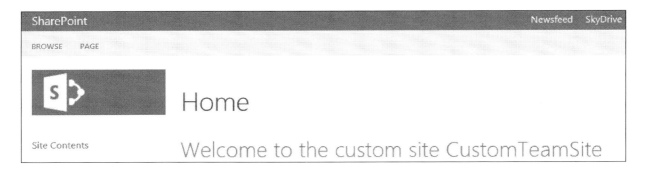

Figure 4.1.3 Instance of a custom site template

For now this is just a blank page, we'll build up this template in a next few scenarios as we add new things to it.

Related scenarios

- *Extending publishing and other site templates*
- *Debugging your SharePoint solution*

4.2 Extending publishing and other site templates

Scenario

In the last scenario we looked at how you can create a new site template which is based of the out-of-the-box Team Site. This time around we'll take a look at how we create publishing and other site templates, to help us build on top of existing functionality available in sites such as wiki sites, community sites, etc.

Set up

We'll be using exactly the same Visual Studio Solution structure as in the previous scenario and since we're building a new site template, you won't need any new site instances pre-created.

Before we begin

In the last scenario, we used an out-of-the-box template and feature definitions as a starting point for our custom Team Site. You may have noticed there are a number of folders at **C:\Program Files\Common Files\microsoft shared\Web Server Extensions\15\TEMPLATE\SiteTemplates**, so what do the rest of the folders represent? How do you determine the one which gives you the base features for the WIKI site, for example? Here are the answers ...

Remember the **webtemp_CustomTeamSite.xml** file which was automatically created in Visual Studio? As it turns out, each template has its own (or shares an existing) template description file. All such files are located here: **C:\Program Files\Common Files\microsoft shared\Web Server Extensions\15\TEMPLATE\1033\XML**.

WEBTEMP.xml for example contains many out-of-the-box template descriptions. Let's open it in Visual Studio or Notepad++.

As you can see, nodes in the file represent templates and the **Name** attribute for each **Template** node represents the corresponding folder name in the template directory (**C:\Program Files\Common Files\microsoft shared\Web Server Extensions\15\TEMPLATE\SiteTemplates**).

Customizing features of your collaboration solution

From here we gather base templates for our main collaboration and publishing sites:

- Publishing Portal

    - Template Description File: **webtempsps.xml**
    - Template Location: **\SiteTemplates\BLANKINTERNET\XML\onet.xml**
    - Configuration: **<Configuration ID="0" Name="BLANKINTERNET">**

- Team Site

    - Template Description File: **webtemp.xml**
    - Template Location: **\SiteTemplates\sts\XML\onet.xml**
    - Configuration: **<Configuration ID="0" Name="Default"** …

- Community Site

    - Template Description File: **webtempsps.xml**
    - Template Location: **\SiteTemplates\COMMUNITY\XML\onet.xml**
    - Configuration: **<Configuration ID="0" Name="Default"** …

- Project Site

    - Template Description File: **webtempsps.xml**
    - Template Location: **\SiteTemplates\PROJECTSITE\XML\onet.xml**
    - Configuration: **<Configuration ID="0" Name="Default"** …

- Enterprise WIKI

    - Template Description File: **webtempsps.xml**
    - Template Location: **\SiteTemplates\ENTERWIKI\XML\onet.xml**
    - Configuration: **<Configuration ID="0" Name="Default"** …

- Enterprise Search Center

    - Template Description File: **webtempsps.xml**

- Template Location: **\SiteTemplates\SRCHCEN\XML\onet.xml**
- Configuration: **<Configuration ID="0" Name="Default"** ...

- Personal Site
    - Template Description File: **webtempsps.xml**
    - Template Location: **\SiteTemplates\SPSMSITEHOST\XML\onet.xml**
    - Configuration: **<Configuration ID="0" Name="Default"** ...

Let's now take a Publishing Portal template and create new instance of it. In this case we're also going to add a custom web part to site template.

How it's done

1. Create new Visual Studio **SharePoint 2013 Empty Project**

2. Specify *http://sp2013* as your debug URL and choose **Deploy as a farm solution** option

3. In the solution explorer, right click on the project name and select **Add | New Item**.... | select **Site Definition** project item

4. Set **CustomPortalSite** as the name for your **Site Definition**

5. In the **CustomPortalSite** project item folder within Visual Studio open the **onet.xml**

6. Open the out-of-the-box version of a publishing portal site template by opening the following path from the server file system:

    C:\Program Files\Common Files\microsoft shared\Web Server Extensions\15\TEMPLATE\SiteTemplates\BLANKINTERNET\XML\onet.xml

7. Locate the section below in the file :

    ```
    <Configuration ID="0" Name="BLANKINTERNET">
    ```

Customizing features of your collaboration solution

8. Copy the nodes, including content, of both **<SiteFeatures>** and **<WebFeatures>** and paste it into the respective areas in the **onet.xml** of our own Visual Studio project, overwriting the existing empty nodes of the same name.

9. We won't be copying the default landing page of the out-of-the-box publishing portal site residing in the **<Module>** since we already have our own blank page

10. Now, let's add out web part project item. In the solution explorer, right click on the project name and select **Add** | **New Item....** | select **Visual Web Part** project item

11. Give our web part a name **PortalWebPart**, and click **Add**

12. You will notice that a new **Feature** has been created in the solution explorer with the name **Feature1**; rename it to **ProvisionWebPart**

13. Open the manifest of **ProvisionWebPart** and copy the **Id**. Also take a note that deployment scope of this feature is set to **Site**, meaning that if we need this feature to be automatically activated with our template it would go into the **<SiteFeatures>** section of our template

14. Switch back to **<SiteFeatures>** section of our custom **onet.xml** file and declare our new feature within the **<SiteFeatures>** node, as follows:

```
<Feature ID="1e8966be-0015-422e-92f9-cd52e0dc7ab4" />
```

Ensure the **Id** here matches the **Id** of the **ProvisionWebPart** feature in your solution

15. To ensure our web part does something, open the **PortalWebPart** folder and **PortalWebPart.ascx** file within it and add the following code:

```
<asp:label ID="label" runat="server"/>
<asp:button ID="button" runat="server" Text="Click me" OnClick="button_Click" />
```

16. Now, open the **PortalWebPart.ascx.cs** file and add the following code right after the **Page_Load** method:

```
protected void button_Click(object sender, EventArgs e)
  {
      label.Text = DateTime.Now.ToString();
  }
```

17. Let's deploy the solution; right click the solution name and click **Deploy**

18. Wait for Visual Studio to finish the solution deployment by following the **Output** windows messages. Navigate back to the **Central Administration** site | under **Application Management** | click **Create site collections**.

19. Fill in the details below:

    a. **Title** – CustomPortalSite
    b. **Url** - CustomPS
    c. **Template Selection** – **SharePoint Customizations** category | **CustomPortalSite**
    d. **Primary Site Collection Administrator** – administrator

20. Click **OK**

Once your site collection is created, add a new page since our landing page doesn't have any web part zones available. Ensure the layout of the new page is **Blank Web Part Page**. When ready, add our **PortalWebPart** web part to one of the existing web part zones. The web part would be located in the **Custom** category. When added, ensure that the custom button function works as expected.

That's all there is to ensure your custom features activate when an instance of the site template is created. Stay tuned to the next few scenarios where we learn how to add lists and list events to your templates.

Related scenarios

- *Extending collaboration site templates*
- *Debugging your SharePoint solution*

Customizing features of your collaboration solution

4.3 Provisioning content pages to your site

Scenario

Provisioning content pages to your site doesn't mean you just need those for testing and then they're gone. You may need to migrate content from one site to another or pre-create content for newly launched section of the site, such as news articles for the news section.

Strictly speaking, you will always need to provision pages with your solution deployment, unless your site is going to be nothing but out-of-the-box sites with the default content; which is highly unlikely.

Set up

We'll be provisioning content pages to both SharePoint collaboration site, a Team Site in our case, and a publishing site. Ensure you have both sites available and as we dive into the code samples, you'll know which one we're working with at that moment.

How it's done

1. Create new Visual Studio **SharePoint 2013 Empty Project**

2. Specify *http://sp2013* as your debug URL and choose **Deploy as a farm solution** option. Ensure the URL you have specified as a debug URL is a site of a Publishing Site template, since we'll start with provisioning content to the site first.

3. In the solution explorer, right click on the project name and select **Add | New Folder | set Pages** as the folder name.

4. Right click on the newly created **Pages** folder | select **Add | New Item....** | select **Module** project item; set **ArticlePage** as the name for your **Module**

5. Rename the **Sample.txt** to **Default.aspx** in the **ArticlePage** module

6. You will notice that a new **Feature** has been created in the solution explorer with the

name **Feature1**; rename it to **ProvisionPages**

7. Open the **Default.aspx** and replace its content with the following code:

```
<%@ Page Inherits="Microsoft.SharePoint.Publishing.TemplateRedirectionPage,Microsoft.SharePoint.Publishing,Version=15.0.0.0,Culture=neutral,PublicKeyToken=71e9bce111e9429c" %>
<%@ Reference VirtualPath="~TemplatePageUrl" %>
<%@ Reference VirtualPath="~masterurl/custom.master" %>
```

The above code will be an instance of our page. This base has a reference to a framework and that's not where the content goes. The content goes into the accompanying XML file along with other page properties, see next step.

8. What your users will see on the page will be defined in the accompanying module XML file. Open the **Elements.xml** and replace its content with the following code:

```
<?xml version="1.0" encoding="utf-8"?>
<Elements xmlns="http://schemas.microsoft.com/sharepoint/">
<Module Name="ArticlePage" Url="Pages" Path="">
<File Url="DemoArticle.aspx" Type="GhostableInLibrary" Path="ArticlePage\default.aspx">
<Property Name="Title" Value="Demo Article Page" />
<Property Name="PublishingPageLayout" Value="~SiteCollection/_catalogs/masterpage/BlankWebPartPage.aspx, Welcome Page;" />
<Property Name="ContentType" Value="$Resources:cmscore,contenttype_welcomepage_name;" />
</File>
</Module>
</Elements>
```

In the code above, we defined a module and a file within the module will be copied over to the **Pages** library of the site this module will be delivered to. The **Pages** is

Customizing features of your collaboration solution

present on each publishing site so as long as we're deploying our module to the publishing site, the page will be copied over.

Among other properties, two important ones are:

PublishingPageLayout – defining the page layout used for this page. If you have provisioned a custom page layout, you're welcome to use it.

ContentType – the content type of the page, in our case we're using a keyword identifying the **Welcome Page**, a default content type available on each publishing site.

9. Let's deploy the solution; right click the solution name and click **Deploy**

10. Wait for the Visual Studio to finish the solution deployment by following the **Output** windows messages. Navigate back to the publishing site *http://sp2013srv*

11. Click **Site Contents** | open the **Pages** library to verify that our custom page named **DemoArticle.aspx** has been created

What if you need to provision several pages? Do we need to create modules for each of them? If all of the pages will end up being deployed to the same page library, it's safe to define their XML in the same module.

Let's see how we can provision another page to our page library using the same Visual Studio solution:

1. In your Visual Studio, open the **Pages** folder | **ArticlePage** module

2. Right click on the **Elements.xml** file and select **Copy**

3. Paste the copied file into the same module and rename the page. In our case, let's call it

    Contact.xml

4. By default, Visual Studio assumes that the file you just pasted is just a content file and, therefore, when compiling, it will ignore the entire markup and not provision your page, even if you define correct parameters in it. Since Visual Studio assumes

you have just added the file and not the XML definition – it's trying to provision a file as content using one of the default modules it created. Select the newly added file and in the file properties window locate the **Deployment Type** property and ensure its value is set to **Element Manifest**

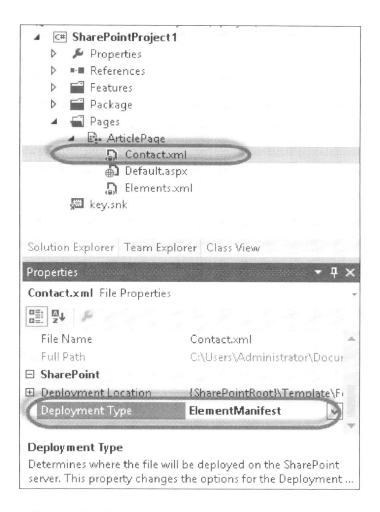

Figure 4.3.1 Changing the deployment type of an item

5. Replace **Contact.xml** content with the following code:

```
<?xml version="1.0" encoding="utf-8"?>
```

Customizing features of your collaboration solution

```
<Elements xmlns="http://schemas.microsoft.com/sharepoint/">
<Module Name="ContactPage" Url="Pages" Path="">
<File Url="Contact.aspx" Type="GhostableInLibrary" Path="ArticlePage\
default.aspx">
<Property Name="Title" Value="Contact Page" />
<Property Name="PublishingPageLayout" Value="~SiteCollection/_
catalogs/masterpage/BlankWebPartPage.aspx, Welcome Page;" />
<Property Name="ContentType" Value="$Resources:cmscore,contenttype_
welcomepage_name;" />
</File>
</Module>
</Elements>
```

Notice how at the beginning of the definition we defined the URL attribute of the file to be **Contact.aspx**; this defines the resulting page name. On the other hand, the **Path** attribute is still pointing to **Default.aspx**; this is source location of where the page is copied from

6. Let's **Deploy** the solution again and after the deployment is complete, navigate to the page library.

7. You should see two custom pages provisioned this time. The process is the same for provisioning additional pages

So far we've looked at how to provision publishing pages; the difference between those and collaboration pages is that there is no **Pages** library for Team Sites, Community Sites, etc. The pages live in what's known as a **root folder**. The provisioning to the root folder is very similar.

Another difference is the fact that collaboration pages don't reference the page layout. Let's take a look at the exact process involved in provisioning collaboration type pages:

1. Create new Visual Studio **SharePoint 2013 Empty Project**

2. Specify *http://sp2013* as your debug URL and choose **Deploy as a farm solution** option. Ensure the URL you have specified as a debug URL is a site of a Team Site

template, since in this case, we're provisioning content to the team site

3. In the solution explorer, right click on the project name and select **Add | New Folder** | set **Pages** as the folder name.

4. Right click on the newly created **Pages** folder | select **Add | New Item**.... | select **Module** project item; set **SimplePage** as the name for your **Module**

5. Delete the **Sample.txt** from the **SimplePage** module

6. You will notice that a new **Feature** has been created in the solution explorer with the name **Feature1**; rename it to **ProvisionPages**

7. Since the Visual Studio SharePoint templates don't include a starter collaboration page, we'll take a bit of a shortcut and get the starter page from the **Site Definition** project item. Right click on the project name in Visual Studio | select **Add | New Item**.... | select **Site Definition** project item

8. Your newly created **site definition** project item will come with several files, one of which **default.aspx**; move the file from this module to the **SimplePage** module

9. Delete the **site definition** project item, we won't need it for anything else

10. Replace the code in **SamplePage | Elements.xml** with the following:

```xml
<?xml version="1.0" encoding="utf-8"?>
<Elements xmlns="http://schemas.microsoft.com/sharepoint/">
<Module Name=" SamplePage">
<File Path=" SamplePage\default.aspx" Url="newpage.aspx" />
</Module>
</Elements>
```

The above code, tells the module to use **default.aspx** page from our solution and copy it to the root of the site (in our case *http://sp2013/newpage.aspx*). In fact, you could use the same module to copy the same **default.aspx** as several different types of pages if you need those few instances of pages on your site

11. Next, open the **default.aspx** from the **SamplePage** module; the code below the reference section will look similar to below:

```
<asp:Content ContentPlaceHolderId="PlaceHolderPageTitle"
runat="server">
    <SharePoint:ProjectProperty Property="Title" runat="server"/>
</asp:Content>

<asp:Content ID="Content1" ContentPlaceHolderId="PlaceHolderMain"
runat="server">
    <h1>
        Welcome to the custom site
        SiteDefinition1
    </h1>
</asp:Content>
```

As you can see, the page will insert a main content into the content area of the default site master page. Unfortunately users won't be even able to change the content on the page because the page doesn't have any controls to be edited, even if users switch in to the edit mode of the page. We'll fix that next.

12. Replace the contents of the **PlaceHolderMain** and add a web part zone instead of just a static text. Here is how our **default.aspx** will look like after this:

```
<asp:Content ContentPlaceHolderId="PlaceHolderPageTitle"
runat="server">
<SharePoint:ProjectProperty Property="Title" runat="server"/>
</asp:Content>

<asp:Content ID="Content1" ContentPlaceHolderId="PlaceHolderMain"
runat="server">
    <WebPartPages:WebPartZone runat="server" Title="Header"
```

```
            ID="Header"/>
        <WebPartPages:WebPartZone runat="server" Title="Main Section"
ID="MainSection"/>
        <WebPartPages:WebPartZone runat="server" Title="Footer"
ID="Footer"/>
</asp:Content>
```

This will add 3 web part zones for users to work with, where they can add web parts containing content and other functionality

13. Let's **Deploy** the solution again and after the deployment is complete, navigate to the root of your team site: *http://sp2013*

14. Now switch the URL to *http://sp2013/newpage.aspx* since we deployed our page directly to the root

15. Our page won't look like much in the display mode, let's switch to the edit mode and ensure all the 3 web part zones are provisioned

In the next scenario we'll take a look at how you can provision default content to web part zones as they're provisioned to the site. This technique will ensure you're not only able to provision the right layout but also some default content to your pages as you deploy your solution.

Related scenarios

- *Extending publishing and other site templates*
- *Provisioning web parts, views and other content to your pages*

4.4 Provisioning web parts, views and other content to your pages

Scenario

In the last scenario we've looked at how you can provision pages to a site. However, thus far the pages have been blank and in most cases that's not acceptable. When you're working on a collaboration site and need to provision base structure to users, you always need to provision a home page, landing pages for main sections and maybe even some initial content pages describing company mission statement, etc. Whether you're using publishing pages or collaboration pages, you need to be able to add some web parts and content on to your pages and in this scenario we'll take a look at how to do exactly that.

Set up

Since we'll be provisioning content pages to both a SharePoint collaboration site and a Team Site, the code sections further in this scenario will explain what type of template we are dealing with to ensure you have the corect site provisioned. To make things simple, ensure you have both, a Team, and a Publishing instance of a site available.

How it's done

1. Open the Visual Studio solution you have created in the previous scenario, and if you haven't already, deploy the solution to the Team Site (*http://sp2013*).

2. Ensure the solution has provisioned a page under the following URL: *http://sp2013/newpage.aspx*. As you remember, this page has 3 web part zones available. We'll be adding a **Content Editor web part** to the zone called **MainSection**

3. To be able to add a web part to a page using Visual Studio, you will need to place a certain declarative XML into a page module. The easiest way to obtain this XML is by adding a web part of your choice manually and letting SharePoint generate the XML for you. Then you can grab it and use it as a basis in your Visual Studio solution.

    a. Navigate to the **newpage.aspx** and switch to edit mode of the page

b. Locate the **Main Section** and click **Add a Web Part**

c. Select **Media and Content** as a web part category | select **Content Editor** as a web part; note, you can pick any web part of your choice | click **Add**

d. Access the web part content menu and select **Export** | save the file offered to the file system. This file contains the declarative XML of the **Content Editor** web part

4. Open the XML file you have saved with Notepad++ or Visual Studio and copy the entire markup to clipboard

5. Switch back to your Visual Studio solution and expand the **SamplePage** module we created in the last scenario

6. Open the **Elements.xml** file which defines where the page is going to be provisioned. We'll add a piece of declarative code from clipboard to the specific part of this file. The XML will provision content editor web part to the web part zone called **MainSection** we have defined in **default.aspx** page

7. Replace the previous content of **Elements.xml** file with this:

```xml
<?xml version="1.0" encoding="utf-8"?>
<Elements xmlns="http://schemas.microsoft.com/sharepoint/">
  <Module Name=" SamplePage">
    <File Path=" SamplePage\default.aspx" Url="newpage.aspx">
      <AllUsersWebPart ID="CEWP" WebPartZoneID="MainSection">
        <![CDATA[
        Web Part XML to be inserted here
        ]]>
      </AllUsersWebPart>
    </File></Module>
</Elements>
```

In the code above we have made few changes; we inserted a new node called

Customizing features of your collaboration solution

`<AllUsersWebPart>` into the `<File>` node. The `<AllUsersWebPart>` has the following attributes:

- **ID** – just a unique identifier of the web part on the page

- **WebPartZoneID** – this identifier has to match exactly the web part zone **ID** in your page; if it doesn't, SharePoint will provision the web part into the first zone it finds

- **WebPartOrder** – you can't see it in the XML here but it's an optional parameter specifying the order of the web part of there is more than one web part in the same zone, which can be the case when you're provisioning few web parts in to a right panel zone, etc.

Next, we have a **CDATA** XML element specifying that the text below is an XML freeform element. This freeform element is going to be our web part declaration.

8. Insert the web part declaration XML you have in your clipboard from step 4 instead of the placeholder text *[Web Part XML to be inserted here]*. Do not delete the outer **CDATA** wrapper.

9. That's it; deploy the solution and navigate to the **newpage.aspx**; you will see the web part automatically provisioned to the page

Now, remember how in the previous scenario: *Provisioning content pages to your site*, right in the first walkthrough of section *How it's done* we provisioned a publishing page, we'll see that the process of provisioning web parts to publishing pages is identical to how it was done just in the previous scenario.

For example, here is the original code we used to provision the page without a web part

```xml
<?xml version="1.0" encoding="utf-8"?>
<Elements xmlns="http://schemas.microsoft.com/sharepoint/">
<Module Name="ArticlePage" Url="Pages" Path="">
<File Url="DemoArticle.aspx" Type="GhostableInLibrary" Path="ArticlePage\default.aspx">
<Property Name="Title" Value="Demo Article Page" />
```

```xml
<Property Name="PublishingPageLayout" Value="~SiteCollection/_
catalogs/masterpage/BlankWebPartPage.aspx, Welcome Page;" />
<Property Name="ContentType" Value="$Resources:cmscore,contenttype_
welcomepage_name;" />
</File>
</Module>
</Elements>
```

And here is the code where we can place the XML declaration of the web part in place of the text *[Web Part XML to be inserted here]*:

```xml
<?xml version="1.0" encoding="utf-8"?>
<Elements xmlns="http://schemas.microsoft.com/sharepoint/">
<Module Name="ArticlePage" Url="Pages" Path="">
<File Url="DemoArticle.aspx" Type="GhostableInLibrary"
Path="ArticlePage\default.aspx">
<Property Name="Title" Value="Demo Article Page" />
<Property Name="PublishingPageLayout" Value="~SiteCollection/_
catalogs/masterpage/BlankWebPartPage.aspx, Welcome Page;" />
<Property Name="ContentType" Value="$Resources:cmscore,contenttype_
welcomepage_name;" />

<AllUsersWebPart ID="CEWP" WebPartZoneID="MainSection">
<![CDATA[
Web Part XML to be inserted here
]]>
</AllUsersWebPart>
</File>
</Module>
</Elements>
```

Final Notes

You probably noticed that the web part declaration XML has a variety of properties, such as `<Title>Content Editor</Title>` for example. Those properties map directly to how the web part behaves. Most of those properties are the same properties you would have access to using SharePoint UI when configuring the web part. Here's a hint: when dealing with a web part you're not too familiar with – add it to the page and configure it using SharePoint UI to match the desired configuration. Then, export the already configured web part to the XML file and use this exported declaration in your code. This will save you time trying our various properties and values directly in XML.

Related scenarios

- *Extending publishing and other site templates*
- *Provisioning content pages to your site*

4.5 Creating SharePoint lists and performing content roll up

Scenario

We've had a quick chance to take a look at SharePoint lists earlier in this book. Calendar, tasks, document libraries and many others are all examples of SharePoint lists. Lists store specific data used by various SharePoint custom and out-of-the-box components. It is not a table in a database but the concept is similar. In this scenario, we'll take a look at how you can provision your own list instance onto the existing SharePoint site and configure an out-of-the-box web part to query content from the list and display it elsewhere on the site.

Set up

If you followed the previous scenario, you're all ready to go. Since lists aren't dependent on the type of the template, you can use any of the existing sites to deploy a list to.

Before we begin

This scenario will have two parts to it. First we'll create a list and deploy it to the existing site and then we'll see how you can have a list provisioned as a part of your custom site template.

It's common that additional lists and libraries actually call for development of a custom site template. Imagine if your site template is used as a project site and project manager would like to have few extra lists available on each new project site. They wouldn't want to create a site and then manually add lists to it; that's when having lists provisioned at the time of site creation becomes a valuable time saver.

How it's done

1. Create a new Visual Studio **SharePoint 2013 Empty Project**

2. Specify *http://sp2013* as your debug URL and choose **Deploy as a farm solution** option

Customizing features of your collaboration solution

3. In the solution explorer, right click on the project name and select **Add | New Folder** | rename the folder to **Lists**

4. Right click on the newly created folder and select **Add | New Item....** | select **List** project item

5. Set **CustomList** as the name for your **List**, click **Add**

6. Here you have two choices, either you create a list instance based on existing list template, such as a calendar list, task list, etc. or you can create a list based on your own template which inherits from a parent. It's very similar to site templates we discussed earlier. We'll create one of each

7. Select **Create a non-customizable list ...** | from the drop down select **Announcements** | click **Finish**

8. A new Feature has been added to the Visual Studio, rename the feature to **ProvisionLists**. This feature will provision both types of lists.

9. Repeat step 4 and 5, but this time give a new list a name **ReallyCustomList** | click **Add**

10. Select **Create a customizable list ...** | from the drop down select **Announcements** | click **Finish**

11. You will see a list of available columns for the list, and you will be able to add new built-in or custom columns too. Notice you haven't been given this option for non-customizable list.

12. Let's add two columns, from the drop down locate the column named **Address** | make the column required. On the next line, type in the name of custom column **BringWithYou**, select type as **Single Line of Text** and mark it as required

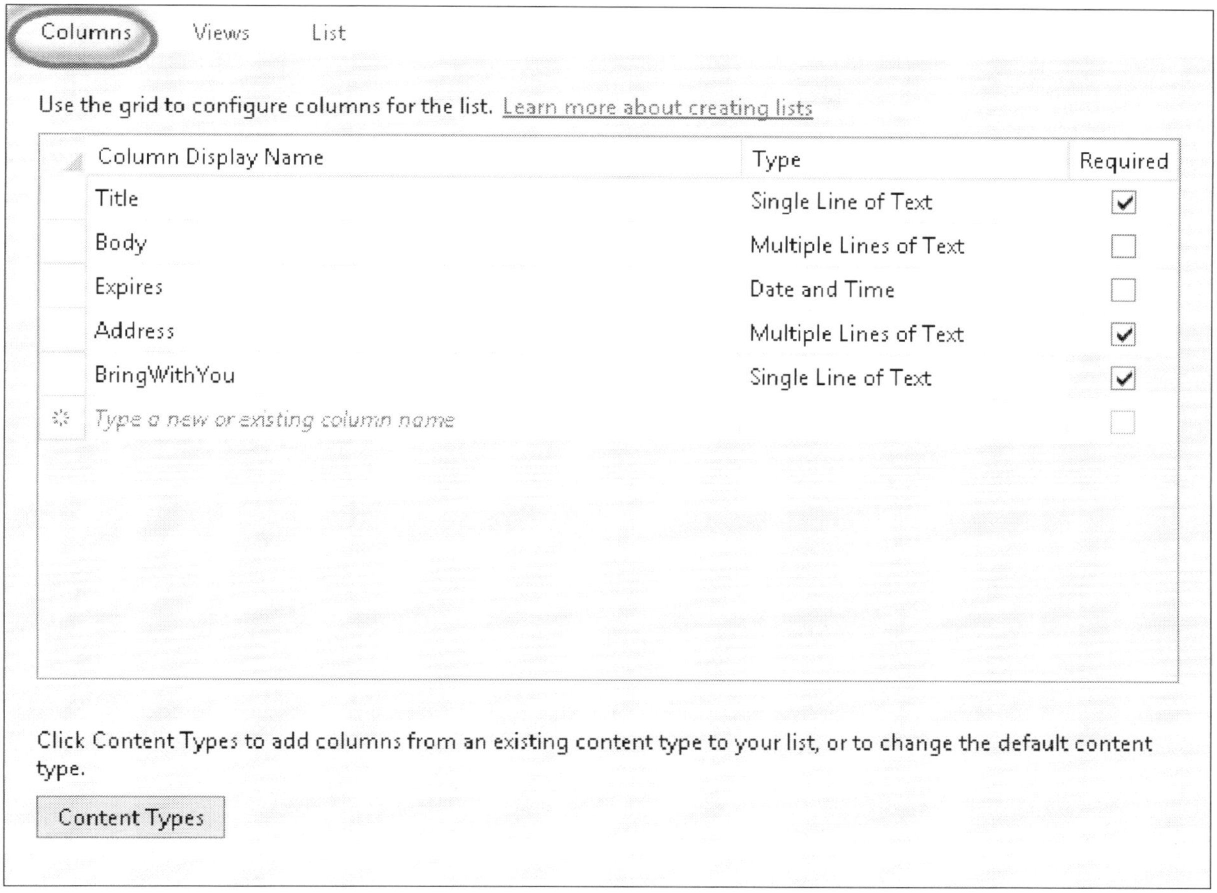

Figure 4.5.1 Adding columns to a custom list

13. Switch to **Views** tab in list editor; in here similarly to columns you can create new views available to users and choose what columns will be visible to users who choose to see the view:

Customizing features of your collaboration solution

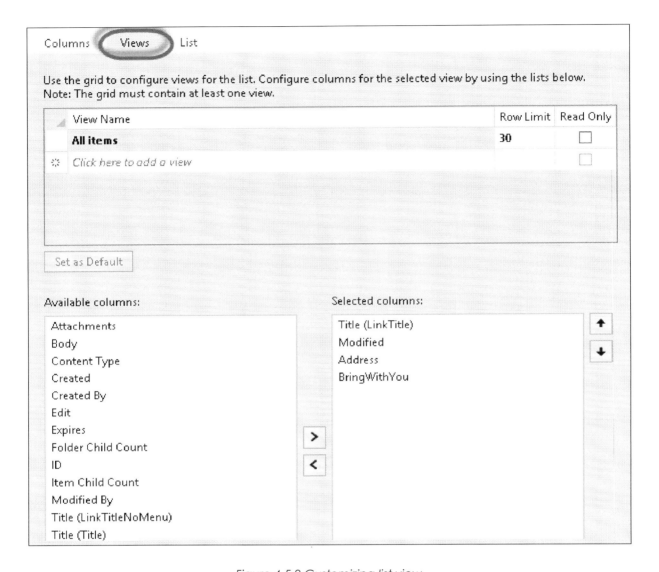

Figure 4.5.2 Customizing list view

14. Create a new view called **CustomView**, select 30 rows limit and add the following columns to the display:

    a. Address
    b. Body
    c. BringWithYou

        d.   Title (LinkTitle)

15. Let's deploy the solution; right click the solution name and click **Deploy**

16. Navigate to the root of our site *http://sp2013* and ensure the site has 2 lists: **CustomList** and **ReallyCustomList**. Choose to add a new item to the list. See how **ReallyCustomList** has additional columns that the list is collecting. Add a new item to the list.

17. From the ribbon select the **List** tab | click the **Current View** drop down | select **CustomView**; notice how only the columns we have specified are displayed in the view

If you wanted those 2 lists to be provisioned as a part of the custom template, you would follow similar steps to deploying a custom web part in the scenario: *Extending publishing and other site templates*. Assuming you would have already added both Site Template and a List to your Visual Studio solution here are the remaining steps to link provisioning of custom list when a site of custom template is being created:

1. Locate below section in the file **onet.xml** file of the custom template:

    ```
    <SiteFeatures>
    ...
    </SiteFeatures>
    ```

2. Open the manifest of the feature which provisions your list, say it's called **ProvisionLists** and copy the **Id**. Also take a note that deployment scope of this feature, we'll assume it's **Site** scoped

3. Switch back to **<SiteFeatures>** section of our custom **onet.xml** file and declare our list provisioning feature within the **<SiteFeatures>** node, as follows:

    ```
    <Feature ID="1e8966be-0015-422e-92f9-cd52e0dc7ab4" />
    ```
    Ensure the **Id** here matches the **Id** of the **ProvisionLists** feature in your solution

4. Deploy the solution; right click the solution name and click **Deploy**

Customizing features of your collaboration solution

5. Wait for the Visual Studio to finish the solution deployment by following the **Output** windows messages. Navigate back to the **Central Administration** site | under **Application Management** | click **Create site collections**

6. Fill in the required details and choose the correct template

7. Click **OK** and wait for the site to be created. Once created, you will see your custom lists deployed along with the site

We have looked at how you can use out-of-the-box rollup web parts to roll up content from lists. Let's take a look at how you can do the same using a custom web part. This will come in handy when you need to customize the look and behavior of your roll up.

1. In the solution explorer of the same solution created earlier in this scenario, right click on the project name and select **Add** | **New Folder** | rename **New Folder** to **WebParts** to keep things organized

2. Right click on the newly created folder and select **Add** | **New Item**…. | select **Visual Web Part** project item

3. Give our web part a name **CustomRollupWebPart**, and click **Add**

4. Add the following reference to the Visual Studio project:

    a. C:\Program Files\Common Files\microsoft shared\Web Server Extensions\15\ISAPI\ Microsoft.SharePoint.Publishing.DLL

5. Open the **CustomRollupWebPart** folder and **CustomRollupWebPart.ascx** file within it and add the following code:

    ```
    <asp:repeater runat="server" ID="MyTable">
    <ItemTemplate>
    <asp:Label ID="Title" runat="server" Text='<%#Eval("Title") %>' />
    </ItemTemplate>
    </asp:repeater>
    ```

    This code will rely on the data source which we'll add next to drive its content

6. Now, open the **CustomRollupWebPart.ascx.cs** file and add the following namespace references:

    a. using Microsoft.SharePoint.Publishing;
    b. using System.Data;
    c. using Microsoft.SharePoint;

7. Add the following code right below the **Page_Load** method; this code will retrieve the data from the site lists:

```
protected virtual DataTable RetrieveData(SPWeb web,
CrossListQueryInfo query)

{
   DataTable resultTable = null;
   CrossListQueryCache queryCache = new CrossListQueryCache(query);
   resultTable = queryCache.GetSiteData(web.Site,
   CrossListQueryCache.ContextUrl());
   return resultTable;
}
```

8. Add the following code right into the **Page_Load** method; this code will define the query according to which we retrieve the data from the site lists:

```
protected void Page_Load(object sender, EventArgs e)
{
   CrossListQueryInfo query = new CrossListQueryInfo();
   query.Query = @"<Where><Eq><FieldRef Name='ContentType' />
   <Value Type='Choice'>ListFieldsContentType</Value>
   </Eq></Where>";
   query.ViewFields = "<FieldRef Name='Title'/>";
```

```
    DataTable table = RetrieveData(SPContext.Current.Web, query);
    MyTable.DataSource = table;
    MyTable.DataBind();
}
```

Above query will parse all items on the site in search for the ones which have our custom content type **ListFieldsContentType**. To find out the name of the custom content type, we navigate to the list in our Visual Studio solution, and in the **Columns** tab | click **Content Types**, the name in bold is the default content type used by items when created

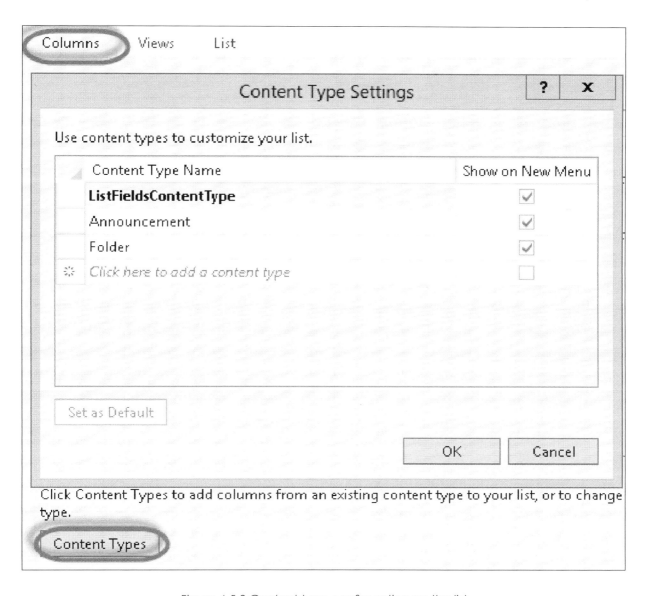

Figure 4.5.3 Content type configuration on the list

We're also retrieving only the **Title** column, in case you need to retrieve other columns, specify their references as below:

```
<FieldRef Name='Title'/>
```

Customizing features of your collaboration solution

```
<FieldRef Name='WorkAddress'/>
<FieldRef Name='BringWithYou'/>
```

Ensure you have referenced those in your ASCX control as well; otherwise the data will be retrieved but not displayed. Also, you'll notice that we referenced **WorkAddress** and not just **Address**, since the internal name of the **Address** column is different from it's display name.

To find out internal name of the column, select it in the column list and check out the Visual Studio item properties as shown below:

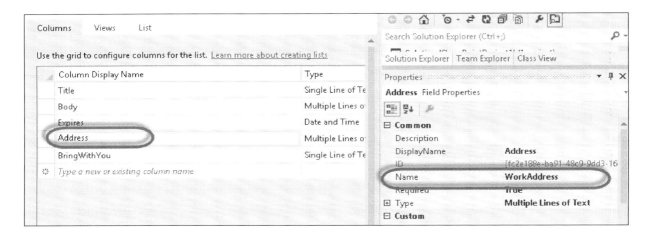

Figure 4.5.4 Discovering internal field names

9. Let's deploy the solution; right click the solution name and click **Deploy**

10. Add a web part to the page, it will be located in the **Custom** web part category and the name of it will be **[Project Name] – CustomRollupWebPart**

11. When deployed, ensure the list has some items added since those get deleted every time you deploy the list. Also, our query results are cached, so when you add new items, give it some time (30 seconds or so) for SharePoint to start recognizing new items in the list.

Here is the result of the query when we add few more columns to the ASCX code, as shown below:

```
<asp:repeater runat="server" ID="MyTable">
<ItemTemplate>
Title:<asp:Label ID="Title" runat="server" Text='<%#Eval("Title") %>'
/><br/>
Address:<asp:Label ID="Label1" runat="server"
Text='<%#Eval("WorkAddress") %>' /><br/>
Bring with you:<asp:Label ID="Label2" runat="server"
Text='<%#Eval("BringWithYou") %>' /><br/>
</ItemTemplate>
</asp:repeater>
```

The output of the web part is the list of two items we have in the list

Related scenarios

- *Capturing list events and executing custom logic on events triggering*

Customizing features of your collaboration solution

4.6 Capturing list events and executing custom logic on events triggering

Scenario

As you interact with your lists and libraries, items in lists trigger events through which you can control whether the user is allowed to add/edit/ or delete an item as well as many other events. There are many scenarios in which you can control what happens to a document in the library or a list item. Since the simplest way to learn about event receiver is to see them in action, let's create one.

Set up

In this scenario we'll be working with document library events so it's handy if you use a Team Site for this example since it already has a document library created by default. Alternatively, you can use any site as long as you create a document library on it. You can also use a Visual Studio solution from the previous scenario and add a new library to it.

How it's done

1. Create a new Visual Studio **SharePoint 2013 Empty Project**

2. Specify *http://sp2013* as your debug URL and choose **Deploy as a farm solution** option

3. In the solution explorer, right click on the project name and select **Add | New Folder | rename the folder to Lists**

4. Right click on the newly created folder and select **Add | New Item.... | select List** project item and set **CustomLibrary** as the name for your **List**, click **Add**

5. Select **Create a non-customizable list ... |** from the drop down select **Document Library |** click **Finish**

6. Right click on the newly created **CustomLibrary** folder, select **Add | New Item... |**

Event Receiver | leave the default name and click **Add**

7. You will be given a choice to determine the type of the receiver. Let's pick **List Item Events**

8. For the event source, Visual Studio will default to our **CustomLibrary**, which is what we want

9. For the events to handle pick: **Item was added**

10. Click **Finish**. You will be taken into the receiver code

11. Replace the **ItemAdded** event method with the following content:

    ```
    public override void ItemAdded(SPItemEventProperties properties)
    {
       if (properties.ListItem.Title.Length < 10)
       {
       properties.ListItem.Delete();
       }
       base.ItemAdded(properties);
    }
    ```

    The method above will get a hold of the current item that fired an event and verify if one of its properties, Title, is less than 10 characters. If so, the event will delete the item.

12. Let's deploy the solution; right click the solution name and click **Deploy**

13. Navigate to the site where the solution has been deployed and open the **CustomLibrary**

14. Upload a new document and when prompted, provide a **Title** for the document ensuring that is has less than 10 characters. Once you confirm the name, the item should be deleted from the list.

Final Notes

The above example demonstrates the logistics of associating an event receiver to a list. One of the common scenarios of event receiver usage is to make the uploaded content only readable to the user who uploaded it. This can be achieved by CheckIn/CheckOut rules in SharePoint or by using a security assignment. By default list items inherit their security from the parent, which is a list or a library.

To ensure that newly uploaded item doesn't inherit the permission assignment from the parent, you can use an event receiver triggered on the item being added. The event receiver would break the security inheritance, with the code below:

```
properties.ListItem.BreakRoleInheritance(false);
```

Essentially, the event receiver is your intermediary layer between SharePoint as it pertains to handling of the items and any custom logic you need to execute on items.

Related scenarios

- *Creating SharePoint lists and performing content roll up*
- *Debugging your SharePoint solution*

4.7 Debugging your SharePoint solution

Scenario

Debugging traditionally refers to troubleshooting your custom code; but in SharePoint it's not just custom code behind web parts and features that can go wrong. Since SharePoint heavily relies on XML declaration to build modules and templates, those components can fail to provision and you would have to troubleshoot exactly why it happened. In this scenario, the set up is pretty simple. We have a custom site template based off the team site, a page module, and a web part. Each time a site template is created, it should contain our custom page with a custom web part on it. We'll have a solution that should do all the provisioning; of course the solution is badly broken. We'll take a look at how you can troubleshoot it so you can learn all the tricks known to man of how to quickly get things back to normal.

Set up

Since debugging isn't limited to a SharePoint site template, let's use a Team Site we created earlier as a debug URL for our Visual Studio solution. Also, copy the code provided in the source code for this scenario. The code contains our crippled solution which we're going to be troubleshooting.

How it's done

1. Open the Visual Studio solution provided with the source code of this scenario and deploy the solution to your debug URL

2. Open the chosen URL in the browser. Since we know that the site template was provisioned, let's try and create a site of our custom site template. Click **Site Contents | + new subsite |** provided **Title** and **Url** as **NewSite |** for **Template Selection** pick **SiteDefinition1** from **SharePoint Customizations**

3. Click **Create** to create a site and you will notice that the site provisioning seemed to have frozen, in about a minute you will get the message similar to below

Customizing features of your collaboration solution

```
Sorry, something went wrong
Cannot complete this action.

Please try again.
Technical Details

Troubleshoot issues with Microsoft SharePoint Foundation.

Correlation ID: 121ddd9b-31ce-f0a0-ed33-e076958e8b9d

Date and Time: 11/1/2012 10:43:06 PM
```

4. Grab the **Correlation ID** and copy it into a clipboard. We'll search SharePoint logs for the correlation ID to find details about the possible error

5. Navigate to **Central Administration | Monitoring | Configure diagnostic logging** | take a note of where the **Trace Logs** are stored. By default the path is : **%CommonProgramFiles%\Microsoft Shared\Web Server Extensions\15\LOGS**

6. Navigate to the path and pick one of the most recent logs or log which modified date correlates with the time where the error occurred

7. Open the file and search for correlation ID you have in clipboard

8. You will find a trace of log for the correlation ID, focus on the ones with **High** severity. Even if you find nothing suspicious, failure to provision the site template means something is wrong with the site template. But in our case we have an error starting with **System.IO.FileNotFoundException**

9. If you take a look at the **onet.xml** of the custom site definition you might see that while copying and pasting the XML of the Team site definition, the developer left the original module from the Team Site definition

```
<Modules>
<Module Name="Default"/>
</Modules>
```

And the module from Visual Studio template

```
<Modules>
<Module Name="DefaultBlank"/>
</Modules>
```

Only one of those modules is actually defined below in the definition – **DefaultBlank** so we need to remove the node:

```
<Modules>
<Module Name="Default"/>
</Modules>
```

10. Save the file and deploy the solution again; repeat steps 1-2 from above. This time the new site is created which means our template has been fixed.

11. Navigate to the custom page which should have a web part provisioned to it *http://sp2013/NewSite/testpage.aspx*. You will find that the page doesn't exist

12. Since the page is provisioned with the module, we need to check the **Elements.xml** of the module to see if the file URL is the one we expect; and it is.

13. Next, we need to make sure that the page module is a part of the feature within our Visual Studio solution; and the module is indeed a part of the feature called **ProvisionWebPart**. It's ok for one feature to provision multiple items. However, as the web part feature is scoped to a **Site** this means that the feature will provision the new page to the root site and not to our custom sub site. So we'll need to create a new feature called **ProvisionPage** and add a **Page** module to it. Also, remove the **Page** module from the **ProvisionWebPart** feature

14. That's not all, we need to ensure the feature containing our module is referenced in the **onet.xml** of our custom template; and it's not there, so the feature is never called and the page would be never provisioned. Create a reference of the feature in your template (Hint: we did something like this in the scenario: *Extending publishing and other site templates*)

15. Let's deploy the solution again. Remember, that just by navigating to *http://sp2013/*

NewSite/testpage.aspx we won't see our changes. The reason being is that since our site instance created earlier was of an old site template which we patched since, we need to create a new site of the same template to see if our changes worked.

16. Repeat steps 1-2 to create new site, this time change the name of the URL to **NewSite2**. Verify whether the custom page is provisioned to the URL: *http://sp2013/NewSite2/testpage.aspx*. The page is there but instead of the web part we get this error:

```
The file you imported is not valid. Verify that the file is a Web Part
description file (*.webpart or *.dwp) and that it contains well-formed
XML.
```

This error means that there is a problem with how the web part was declared on the page. If you remember the trick to getting the web part declaration XML from the scenario: *Provisioning web parts, views and other content to your pages*, that would be the easiest and least error prone way to get the declaration XML, so what happened?

17. Open the **Page | Elements.xml** and take a look at the title property:

```
<property name="Title" type="string">Lists & Libraries</property>
```

At first glance, it seems like there is nothing wrong with it. However, declaration XML doesn't like it when you use special characters such as the **&** in property values. Those need to be encoded into HTML entities, so **&** becomes **&**

Our solution developer might have copied the XML using a technique described earlier, but then they decided to change the title of the web part. This is a common mistake for developers to make. So let's switch the illegal character to an encoded one.

18. Deploy the solution again and create a new site just as before.

19. We now have a page and a web part which displays list titles from the current site and we haven't even gotten to the web part .NET code

20. Let's see how we can debug web part .NET code.

21. Ensure your solution has been deployed and you accessed the page where the web part resides at least once

22. In Visual Studio, in the top menu click **Debug** | **Attach to Process** | in the proposed window select **Show processes from all users** | select all instances on **w3wp.exe** process | click **Attach** | confirm attaching to each of the processes

23. Open the **VisualWebPart1.ascx.cs** file and place a break point in a piece of code which you intend to debug, in our case at the beginning of *Page_Load* method. When you refresh the page next, your breakpoint will fire and you can start debugging the code

Related scenarios

- *Extending publishing and other site templates*
- *Provisioning web parts, views and other content to your pages*

Customizing features of your collaboration solution

4.8 Customizing SharePoint structured and managed navigation

Scenario

SharePoint comes with a set of default navigation controls allowing users to navigate the site. As you have seen from previous scenarios, there are quite few navigation controls available to users.

There is a suite bar available on each page and site, there is a global navigation usually hovering on the top of the page, and there is quick launch navigation typically on the left hand side of the page.

Most of those controls are configurable and can be extended to fit your need. In this scenario, we'll see exactly what's involved in manipulating the behavior of out-of-the-box navigation controls.

Set up

In this scenario we'll be working with a publishing site template so ensure you have created a site collection of a publishing site template. To check out how to create it, see scenario: *Publishing Portal | How to create it*

Before we begin

SharePoint 2013 publishing site has two types of navigation: structured driven navigation and managed metadata driven navigation. We've discussed before, structured driven navigation will be built up from sites and pages. As you add more pages and sub sites, those will be added to the navigation hierarchy. There is also a configuration interface which allows users to hide any pages from navigation. To access this configuration, do the following:

1. Select the site where they have unwanted pages displayed on the top navigation and click the **Gear Menu | Site Settings**

2. From the settings page, click the **Navigation** link located under the **Look and Feel** category

3. From there you can choose whether pages are shown at all on the site as well as pick individual pages and hide them from the navigation.

You can also drive the navigation of the site entirely using managed metadata structure defined in Central Administration. This way your pages are independent of the structure and you can always change the navigation without touching the site structure. We've seen how you can build managed metadata structure in this scenario: *Enterprise WIKI | Collaboration essentials | Configuring WIKI categories*

How it's done

First let's take a look at how we can leverage the structured navigation when defining a new site template. We've looked at how to create a new site template few scenarios earlier in: *Extending publishing and other site templates*

When creating a new publishing site template based on the existing site template, we've come across a **WebFeature** with the following definition:

```
<Feature ID="541F5F57-C847-4e16-B59A-B31E90E6F9EA">
<!-- Per-Web Portal Navigation Properties-->
<Properties xmlns="http://schemas.microsoft.com/sharepoint/">
<Property Key="InheritGlobalNavigation" Value="true"/>
<Property Key="IncludeSubSites" Value="true"/>
<Property Key="IncludePages" Value="false"/>
</Properties>
</Feature>
```

If you're ever interested where the feature is defined, follow this location: [Drive]:\Program Files\Common Files\Microsoft Shared\Web Server Extensions\15\TEMPLATE\FEATURES\NavigationProperties.

There are actually few more properties to this feature than the ones defined in the publishing

Customizing features of your collaboration solution

site **onet.xml**. Here is the complete list of accepted properties and their sample values:

```xml
<Feature ID="541F5F57-C847-4e16-B59A-B31E90E6F9EA">
<!-- Per-Web Portal Navigation Properties-->
<Properties xmlns="http://schemas.microsoft.com/sharepoint/">
<Property Key="InheritGlobalNavigation" Value="true" />
<Property Key="InheritCurrentNavigation" Value="true" />
<Property Key="ShowSiblings" Value="true" />
<Property Key="IncludeSubSites" Value="true" />
<Property Key="IncludePages" Value="true" />
<Property Key="GlobalIncludeSubSites" Value="true" />
<Property Key="GlobalIncludePages" Value="true" />
<Property Key="CurrentIncludeSubSites" Value="true" />
<Property Key="CurrentIncludePages" Value="true" />
<Property Key="GlobalDynamicChildLimit" Value="99" />
<Property Key="CurrentDynamicChildLimit" Value="99" />
<Property Key="OrderingMethod" Value="Automatic" />
<Property Key="AutomaticSortingMathod" Value="LastModifiedDate" />
<Property Key="SortAscending" Value="true" />
<Property Key="IncludeInGlobalNavigation" Value="true" />
<Property Key="IncludeInCurrentNavigation" Value="true" />
</Properties>
</Feature>
```

Most all of the values are descriptive and are mapped to the options available in the users interface which means you can easily reference the SharePoint navigation configuration page to get equivalent configuration using a feature.

The above applies when you're creating a brand new template from which sites are going to be built, but what if you already have a site and now you need to change how the navigation behaves in a structured navigation scenario? Let's see how we can create a custom Visual Studio solution which does exactly that.

1. Create new Visual Studio **SharePoint 2013 Empty Project**

2. Specify *http://sp2013* as your debug URL and choose **Deploy as a farm solution** option

3. In the solution explorer, right click on the folder named **Features** | **Add Feature**

4. Set **HidePagesFromNavigation** as the name for your feature

5. Right click on the newly created feature folder | select **Add Event Receiver**

6. Add a new project reference assembly called **Microsoft.SharePoint.Publishing** to facilitate using the publishing framework in our solution

7. Open the newly created feature event received code file: **HidePagesFromNavigation.EventReceiver.cs** and add a new namespace reference to your feature: *using Microsoft.SharePoint.Publishing*

8. Locate the **Feature_Activated** method of the receiver and replace the code of the method with the following:

```
public override void FeatureActivated(SPFeatureReceiverProperties properties)
{
   using (SPWeb web = properties.Feature.Parent as SPWeb)
   {
   PublishingWeb pw = Microsoft.SharePoint.Publishing.PublishingWeb.GetPublishingWeb(web);
   pw.Navigation.InheritGlobal = true;
   pw.Navigation.ShowSiblings = true;
   pw.Navigation.OrderingMethod = OrderingMethod.Automatic;
   pw.Navigation.SortAscending = true;
   pw.Update();
```

Customizing features of your collaboration solution

```
SPQuery query = new SPQuery();
query.ViewFields = "<FieldRef Name='Title' />";
query.Query = @"<Where><Contains><FieldRef Name='Title'/>
<Value Type='Text'>Contact Page</Value>
</Contains></Where>";
SPListItemCollection itemCollection = pw.PagesList.
GetItems(query);
if (itemCollection.Count > 0)
{
PublishingPage contactPage = PublishingPage.GetPublishingPage(item
Collection[0]);
contactPage.IncludeInGlobalNavigation = true;
}
}
}
```

The code above contains two examples, in the first part of the code we get a hold of the current

publishing web and set its navigation properties just as we did using a publishing feature XML.

In the second part, we get a hold of an individual page on the site titled *Contact Page* and set it to be included in the global navigation. See, pages decide whether they will surface in the global navigation data source, so in order to make them invisible or visible, you need to get a hold of the page itself

9. Ensure you have created a new page with the title *Contact Page* and deploy the Visual Studio solution. When deployed, the solution will activate the feature and set your configuration settings as requested.

So far we looked at how to manipulate structured navigation; which involves quite a bit of work compare to the flexibility of managed navigation. With managed navigation you create a navigation structure in Central Administration managed metadata term store and map each menu item to a URL. As you see a need for change you can move around managed metadata terms and their relationship in hierarchy will change without a need to change actual page and site structure. This is a new approach in SharePoint which is also embraced in many other content management systems.

Let's take a look at how you can build a simple structure and set a site to use managed metadata navigation.

First, let's ensure your environment has managed metadata service enabled:

1. Navigate to the Central Administration home page

2. Under **System Settings** | click **Manage services on server**

3. Ensure that **Managed Metadata Web Service** is **Started**

4. Next, navigate back to the Central Administration home page and this time select **Application Management** | **Manage service applications**

5. Ensure you have a **Managed Metadata** service application created which is identified by the **Type** column in the list as **Managed Metadata Web Service**

6. If you do not have a **Managed Metadata** service application created, click the **New** button in the ribbon and select **Managed Metadata Service**; provide at least the following non-default values:

    a. **Name**: ManagedMetadata

    b. **Database Name**: ManagedMetadata

    c. **Application pool name**: ManagedMetadata

   All the other settings can be left as set by default; click OK and let the service application be created

7. Verify that the Managed Metadata service application is created; navigate to the **Manage service application page** | click the link for the newly created **ManagedMetadata** | The term store management tool should look similar to below

Customizing features of your collaboration solution

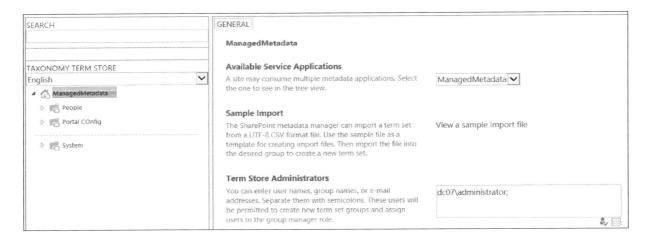

Figure 4.8.1 Term store management tool

Next, let's create our Visual Studio solution to drive the publishing site navigation using managed metadata

1. Create new Visual Studio **SharePoint 2013 Empty Project**

2. Specify *http://sp2013* as your debug URL and choose **Deploy as a farm solution** option

3. In the solution explorer, right click on the folder named **Features | Add Feature**

4. Set **SetUpManagedNavigation** as the name for your feature

5. Right click on the newly created feature folder | select **Add Event Receiver**

6. Add two new project reference assemblies:

    a. **Microsoft.SharePoint.Publishing** - to facilitate using the publishing framework in our solution

    b. **Microsoft.SharePoint.Taxonomy** – to facilitate work with taxonomy term sets in Central Administration

7. Open the newly created feature event received code file: **SetUpManagedNavigation.EventReceiver.cs** and add few new namespace

reference to your feature:

   a. *using Microsoft.SharePoint.Publishing*
   b. *using Microsoft.SharePoint.Publishing.Navigation*
   c. *using Microsoft.SharePoint.Taxonomy*

8. Locate the **Feature_Activated** method of the receiver and add the following code right below it:

```
private TermStore ProvisionTermsStructure(SPWeb web)
{
   TaxonomySession session = new TaxonomySession(web.Site);
   TermStore store = session.TermStores["ManagedMetadata"];
   TermSetCollection collection = store.GetTermSets("NavTermSet",
   1033);
   if (collection != null && collection.Count == 0)
   {
   Group group = store.CreateGroup("PublishingNav");
   TermSet termSet = group.CreateTermSet("NavTermSet");
   Term term1 = termSet.CreateTerm("Nav Item 1", 1033);
   term1.CreateTerm("Sub Term 1", 1033);
   termSet.CreateTerm("Nav Item 2", 1033);
   store.CommitAll();
   }
   return store;
}
```

The code above accesses the **ManagedMetadata** taxonomy store in Central Administration and provisions the custom group called **PublishingNav**. Below this group, we create a custom term set called **NavTermSet**. Finally, we create two new terms and save our changes.

You'll notice we used 1033 constant to represent locale ID for English/US. For a

Customizing features of your collaboration solution

complete list of locale IDs search MSDN with the keyword *Locale IDs*.

9. Locate the **Feature_Activated** method of the receiver and replace the code of the method with the following:

```
public override void FeatureActivated(SPFeatureReceiverProperties properties)
{
   using (SPWeb web = properties.Feature.Parent as SPWeb)
   {
   TermStore store = ProvisionTermsStructure(web);

   PublishingWeb pw = Microsoft.SharePoint.Publishing.PublishingWeb.
   GetPublishingWeb(web);
   WebNavigationSettings navSettings = new WebNavigationSettings(web);

   navSettings.GlobalNavigation.Source = StandardNavigationSource.
   TaxonomyProvider;
   navSettings.GlobalNavigation.TermStoreId = store.Id;
   TermSetCollection termSetCol = store.GetTermSets("NavTermSet",
   1033);
   if (termSetCol.Count > 0)
   {
   navSettings.GlobalNavigation.TermSetId = termSetCol[0].Id;
   }
   navSettings.AddNewPagesToNavigation = true;
   navSettings.CreateFriendlyUrlsForNewPages = true;
   navSettings.Update();
   pw.Update();
   }
}
```

The code above references our custom function, **ProvisionTermsStructure**, which provisions the navigation terms into the term store. Once the terms are provisioned into the term store we associate the data source of the navigation to use the term store. We provide the Id of the term store and the term set. Any items below the specified term set will be interpreted as navigation elements.

10. Deploy the solution using Visual Studio and navigate to the root of your publishing site we used for deployment; the navigation should look as shown below:

Figure 4.8.2 Managed term store driven navigation

Customizing features of your collaboration solution

11. Navigate to the navigation settings page, the configuration will look as below:

Figure 4.8.3 Navigation configured with a term store

Chapter 4

12. Finally, here is how the managed metadata term store will look like after the provisioning of our custom items:

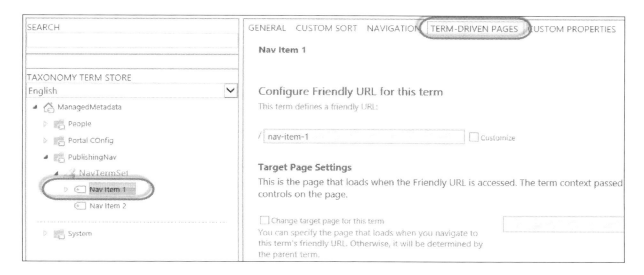

Figure 4.8.4 Term driven navigation configuration within a term store

You'll notice that each term, when clicked will have several tabs on the right on the term tree. One of the important options is in the tab called **Term-Drive Pages**, the option here **Target Page Settings** will define the exact URL of the page which a particular item is assigned to.

The pages must exist before you assign navigation terms to them. In a typical scenario, you would provision your **Managed Metadata** tree after the pages are provisioned and then assign the URL to each term

Related scenarios

- *Customizing SharePoint 2013 suite bar menu*

Customizing features of your collaboration solution

4.9 Customizing SharePoint 2013 suite bar menu

Scenario

In the last scenario we've looked at how you can customize main SharePoint navigation. There is another type of navigation control in SharePoint, the suite bar. The difference between the suite bar and other types of navigation is that suite bar will appear everywhere on the site no matter which sub site or page you navigate to. It has some handy out-of-the-box links; however, one of the most common requests is to add your own site links, such as the link to root portal, or central administration (if the user is an administrator) or some other important corporate tool that deserves enough attention to be right on the top of every page. You can even customize what your suite bar will show based on the user preferences or permissions. In this scenario, we'll take a look how you can extend your suite bar to facilitate other links.

Set up

Since the suite bar shows up on every page, regardless of the template, we'll use our team site as a debug/development site, but you're welcome to use a site of your choice

Before we begin

The suite bar is inserted into a master page placeholder called **SuiteBarBrandingDelegate**. Each master page is required to have one so that suite bar is inserted into the placeholder.

```
<SharePoint:DelegateControl id="ID_SuiteBarBrandingDelegate" Control
Id="SuiteBarBrandingDelegate" runat="server" />
```

Placing a delegate control definition above is a common method for many out-of-the-box and custom controls to be inserted into the required place on a master page and suite bar is no exception. What we'll do next, is we'll create a user control in our Visual Studio and register this user control as a delegate control to be inserted into a master page placeholder.

Delegate controls use sequence IDs to determine the order they will be inserted. The lower the number assigned to the Delegate control, the higher it's priority; we'll ensure that out custom control is inserted right before out-of-the-box suite bar is.

You might think that just replacing the out-of-the-box suite bar is not enough, after all, we want the out-of-the-box suite bar behavior, plus we want to add few more links of our own. And you're right. We won't just replace the suite bar, we'll inherit its functionality and add extra logic. This approach will ensure our customization doesn't break any existing dependencies or future enhancements to suite bar. We'll just let the suite bar do its job and render our links after.

How it's done

1. Create new Visual Studio **SharePoint 2013 Empty Project**

2. Specify *http://sp2013* as your debug URL and choose **Deploy as a farm solution** option

3. In the solution explorer, right click on the folder named **Features** | **Add Feature**

4. Set **ProvisionSuiteBar** as the name for your feature

5. Open the feature properties page to change its scope to **Farm**. By changing the scope to farm we ensure that the customization is applied to each site on the farm which is very appropriate to suite bar since it's present everywhere on the SharePoint farm

6. Right click the project name and add a new project item: **Add** | **New Item ...** | **User Control** | name it **CustomSuiteBar.ascx** | click **Add**

7. Ensure the project has the following assembly reference:

    a. C:\Program Files\Common Files\microsoft shared\Web Server Extensions\15\ISAPI\Microsoft.Sharepoint.Portal.dll

8. Switch to the newly created user control code file **CustomSuiteBar.ascx.cs** and add the following namespace references:

Customizing features of your collaboration solution

      a. using Microsoft.SharePoint;

      b. using Microsoft.SharePoint.Portal.WebControls;

9. Change the class for our **CustomSuiteBar** user control to inherit from **MySuiteLinksUserControl** as below:

```
public partial class CustomSuiteBar : MySuiteLinksUserControl
```

This will ensure that our new class has all of the functionality of its parent, the real-deal, out-of-the-box suite bar

10. Open the **CustomSuiteBar.ascx.cs** file accompanying the user control we've just added, and add the following method right after the **Page_Load**:

```
protected override void Render(HtmlTextWriter writer)
{
   writer.RenderBeginTag(HtmlTextWriterTag.Style);
   writer.Write(".ms-core-suiteLinkList {display: inline-block;}");
   writer.RenderEndTag();
   writer.AddAttribute(HtmlTextWriterAttribute.Class, "ms-core-suiteLinkList");
   writer.RenderBeginTag(HtmlTextWriterTag.Ul);
   RenderSuiteLink(writer, "/", "Home", "HomeLink", false);
   writer.RenderEndTag();
   base.Render(writer);
}
```

Since our custom control is actually a child of the out-of-the-box suite bar, we can intercept its *Render* method to render anything custom we desire before out-of-the-box links get rendered. In our case we'll render the link to a root site. To make sure that out link is on the same line with the rest of the links, we add an **inline-block** attribute on both out custom links and out-of-the-box suite bar

11. Next, we need to ensure that the custom suite bar is added to all sites . Right click on the project name and add a new project item: **Add** | **New Item ...** | **Empty Element**

| name it **SuiteBarDelegate** | click **Add**

12. Open the accompanying **Elements.xml** file and replace its contents with the following:

```
<?xml version="1.0" encoding="utf-8"?>
<Elements xmlns="http://schemas.microsoft.com/sharepoint/">
<Control Id="SuiteLinksDelegate" Sequence="90" ControlSrc="~/_ControlTemplates/15/SharePointProject1/CustomSuiteBar.ascx" />
</Elements>
```

Above will ensure that the new user control **CustomSuiteBar.ascx** is referenced on all farm master pages in a placeholder called **SuiteLinksDelegate**. The sequence value of **90** will make sure the reference happens before the out of the box suite bar is called (its defaut sequence value is 100)

13. The newly added element will be added to our feature: **ProvisionSuiteBar**

14. Deploy the solution using Visual Studio and navigate to any of your SharePoint sites to make sure our custom suite bar is rendered with an extra link before the rest of the links:

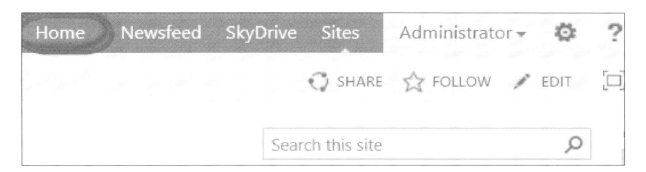

Figure 4.9.1 Custom suite bar on the page

Related scenarios

- Customizing SharePoint structured and managed navigation
- Using user profile property values in your solution

4.10 Working with user profiles and user profile properties

Scenario

We've briefly looked at the user profiles when discussing *Personal Site | Manage its content*. Personal sites use user profiles to store individual user information. This information is stored in a designated profile database. You can access user profile information from within custom built and existing out-of-the-box components. Profiles hold the information in a collection of user profile properties and you can add new properties to store your specific solution information. The whole purpose of the user profiles is to store relevant information for a currently logged in user. Storing your custom solution information pertaining to a given user allows you to change the behavior of your web parts and other controls to render depending on the user profile data.

Set up

The user profile system depends on the **User Profile Service Application**. If you're using a pre-configured SharePoint 2013 development environment from CloudShare, you will have a configured instance of this service application. Otherwise, search TechNet with the following keyword: *SharePoint 2013: Setting up a MySite - User Profile Service*

Before we begin

Once your User Profile Service Application is configured and running, you will be able to see user profiles of users you have added in your SharePoint system, those are likely to be administrative users required to run the farm.

Let's take a look at the user profiles currently available on your system using SharePoint Central Administration:

1. Navigate to the home page of your Central Administration and under **Application Management** | click **Manage service applications**

2. Find the service application in the list which **Type** value is **User Profile Service Application**; click on the link representing this service application

3. On the service application page, under **People** group | click **Manage user profiles**

4. Search for an existing user, in our case *administrator*. In the search results, access the context menu of the user and click **Edit My Profile**. The list of profile properties you see are all out-of-the-box properties. We'll take a look at how you can add your own in the following scenario. Now let's see how you can create your own profile programmatically with Visual Studio

How it's done

1. Create new Visual Studio **SharePoint 2013 Empty Project**

2. Specify *http://sp2013* as your debug URL and choose **Deploy as a farm solution** option

3. In the solution explorer, right click on the folder named **Features** | **Add Feature**

4. Set **ProvisionProfiles** as the name for your feature and set its scope to **Site**

5. Add a new event receiver to a feature and switch to its code file : **ProvisionProfiles.EventReceiver.cs**

6. Add the following assembly references to the solution:

    a. *Microsoft.Office.Server.UserProfiles.dll*

    b. *Microsoft.SharePoint.Portal.dll*

    c. *Microsoft.SharePoint.Taxonomy.dll*

    d. *System.Web.dll*

    e. *Microsoft.Office.Server.dll*

7. Also, add the following namespace references to the receiver code:

    a. *using Microsoft.Office.Server.UserProfiles;*

    b. *using Microsoft.SharePoint.Taxonomy;*

    c. *using System.Web;*

    d. *using Microsoft.SharePoint.WebControls;*
    e. *using Microsoft.SharePoint.Portal.WebControls;*
    f. *using Microsoft.Office.Server;*

8. Replace the **FeatureActivated** method of the receiver with the following code:

```
public override void FeatureActivated(SPFeatureReceiverProperties properties)
{
   SPSite siteColl = properties.Feature.Parent as SPSite;
   SPServiceContext serviceContext = SPServiceContext.GetContext(siteColl);
   UserProfileManager userProfileManager = new UserProfileManager(serviceContext);
   UserProfile newProfile = userProfileManager.CreateUserProfile([Account], [Account]);
   newProfile[PropertyConstants.WorkPhone].Add("555-555-5555");
   newProfile[PropertyConstants.Department].Add("Marketing");
   newProfile[PropertyConstants.Title].Add("Chief");
   newProfile[PropertyConstants.DistinguishedName].Add([Account]);
   newProfile[PropertyConstants.Office].Add("Western Branch");
   newProfile.Commit();
   siteColl.Dispose();
}
```

The above code will create a new profile and set some of the basic out-of-the-box properties. One property you will need to change is the User Id. This property is already installed on your system and in our code its value is set to *[Account]*. If on your test system you have only one account, you can delete its profile using Central Administration interface or using Visual Studio

9. To remove the profile before it's created, add the following code before the provisioning code in **FeatureActivated**:

Customizing features of your collaboration solution

```
public override void FeatureActivated(SPFeatureReceiverProperties
properties)
{
   SPSite siteColl = properties.Feature.Parent as SPSite;
   SPServiceContext serviceContext = SPServiceContext.
   GetContext(siteColl);
   UserProfileManager userProfileManager = new UserProfileManager(servic
   eContext);
   UserProfile existingProfile = userProfileManager.
   GetUserProfile(@"domain\[Account]");
   if (existingProfile != null)
   {
   userProfileManager.RemoveUserProfile(existingProfile.ID);
   }
   UserProfile newProfile = userProfileManager.
   CreateUserProfile([Account], [Account]);
   // ...truncated code from above...
   newProfile.Commit();
   diteColl.Dispose();
}
```

The above will come in handy as you're running the solution a few times while testing the code

10. Deploy the solution using Visual Studio

11. To verify that our profile was created navigate to the home page of your Central Administration and under **Application Management** | click **Manage service applications**

12. Find the **User Profile Service Application** and under **People** group | click **Manage user profiles**

13. Search for an existing user and the context menu of the user and click **Edit My Profile**. The list of profile property values you see should be all the property values we set in our code

Related scenarios

- *Creating custom user profile properties*

4.11 Creating custom user profile properties

Scenario

As you've seen in the previous scenario, user profile properties store a lot of data and there is a good chance that if you need to store user contextual data – user profiles is the best place to use. After all, you can access to the user profile data of the currently logged in user and change the execution logic according to your needs, making your solution adaptable and user friendly. In this scenario, we'll see how you can provision a custom user profile property to save specific solution information and also how to access this information within our custom component

Before we begin

First, before we start creating new properties, let's take a look where the properties are defined and managed in Central Administration:

1. Navigate to the home page of your Central Administration and under **Application Management** | click **Manage service applications**

2. Find a service application in the list which **Type** value is **User Profile Service Application**; click on the link representing this service application

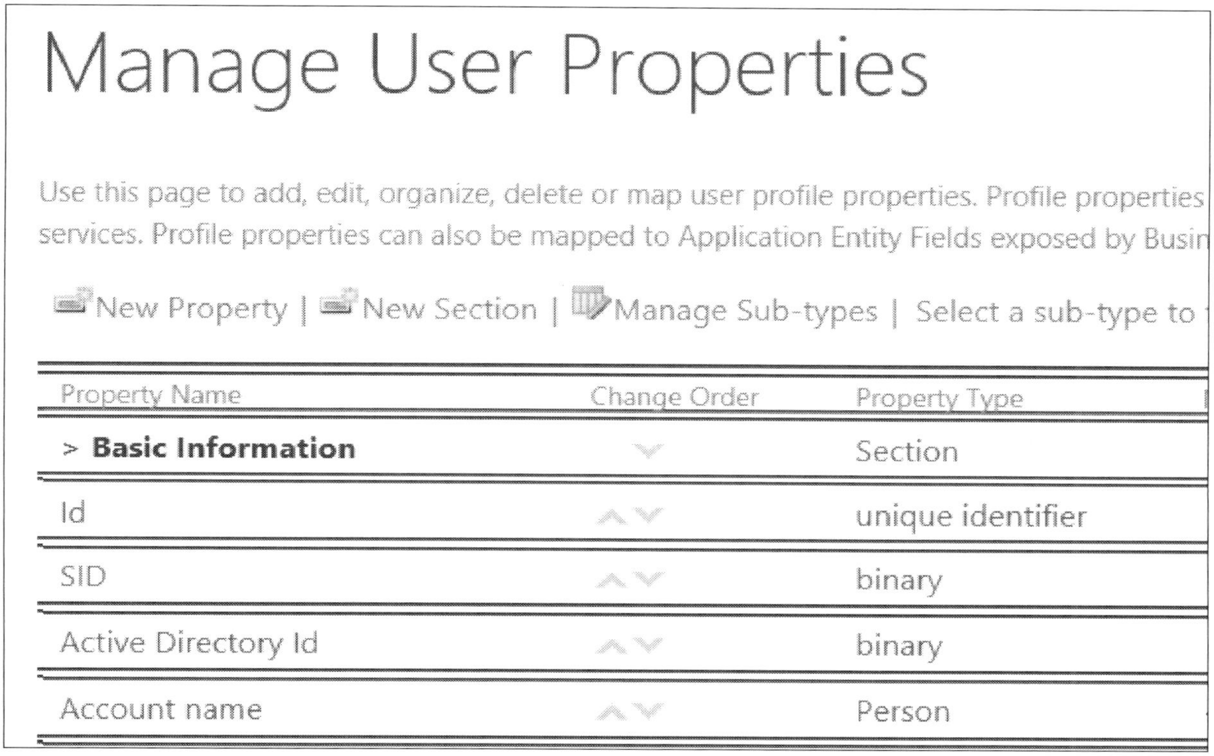

Manage User Properties

Use this page to add, edit, organize, delete or map user profile properties. Profile properties services. Profile properties can also be mapped to Application Entity Fields exposed by Busin

New Property | New Section | Manage Sub-types | Select a sub-type to

Property Name	Change Order	Property Type
> **Basic Information**	∨	Section
Id	∧∨	unique identifier
SID	∧∨	binary
Active Directory Id	∧∨	binary
Account name	∧∨	Person

Figure 4.11.1 User profile properties

3. On the service application page, under **People** group | click **Manage user properties**

   You will see a list of all the available properties and their types.

You'll notice—depending on the type you will have access to—different parameters within the property configuration page. For example, take a look at the **About Me** property. Open the Edit menu. Check out some of the values and compare them with another property in the list, say **Interests**.

You will notice that the first property is a simple text property, where **Interests** has additional options since this property saves metadata type of information where users can type one or more interests that will be stored in the metadata store we looked at earlier.

Now let's see how you can create your own profile programmatically with Visual Studio.

Customizing features of your collaboration solution

How it's done

1. Create a new Visual Studio **SharePoint 2013 Empty Project**

2. Specify *http://sp2013* as your debug URL and choose **Deploy as a farm solution** option

3. In the solution explorer, right click on the folder named **Features | Add Feature**

4. Set **ProvisionProfileProperties** as the name for your feature and set its scope to **Site**

5. Add a new event receiver to a feature and switch to its code file : **ProvisionProfileProperties.EventReceiver.cs**

6. Add the following assembly references to the solution:

    a. *Microsoft.Office.Server.UserProfiles.dll*
    b. *Microsoft.SharePoint.Portal.dll*
    c. *Microsoft.SharePoint.Taxonomy.dll*
    d. *System.Web.dll*
    e. *Microsoft.Office.Server.dll*

7. Also, add the following namespace references to the receiver code:

    a. *using Microsoft.Office.Server.UserProfiles;*
    b. *using Microsoft.SharePoint.Taxonomy;*
    c. *using Microsoft.SharePoint.WebControls;*
    d. *using System.Web;*
    e. *using Microsoft.SharePoint.Portal.WebControls;*
    f. *using System.Collections.Generic;*
    g. *using System.Diagnostics;*

8. Replace the **FeatureActivated** method of the receiver with the following code:

```
public override void FeatureActivated(SPFeatureReceiverProperties
```

```
properties)
{
   SPSite siteColl = properties.Feature.Parent as SPSite;
   SPServiceContext serviceContext =
   SPServiceContext.GetContext(siteColl);
   UserProfileConfigManager upcm =
   new UserProfileConfigManager(serviceContext);
   ProfileSubtypeManager psm =
   ProfileSubtypeManager.Get(serviceContext);
   ProfileSubtype ps = psm.GetProfileSubtype(ProfileSubtypeManager.
   GetDefaultProfileName(ProfileType.User));
   ProfileSubtypePropertyManager pspm = ps.Properties;


   ProfilePropertyManager ppm = upcm.ProfilePropertyManager;
   CorePropertyManager cpm = ppm.GetCoreProperties();

   try
   {
   CoreProperty cp = cpm.Create(false); ;

   cp.Name = "MyProperty";
   cp.DisplayName = "My Property";
   cp.Description = "My Property";
   cp.Type = "string";
   cp.IsMultivalued = true;
   cp.IsSearchable = true;
   cp.Length = 100;
   cpm.Add(cp);

   ProfileTypePropertyManager ptpm =
```

Customizing features of your collaboration solution

```
        ppm.GetProfileTypeProperties(ProfileType.User);
        ProfileTypeProperty ptp = ptpm.Create(cp);
        ptp.IsVisibleOnEditor = true;
        ptp.IsVisibleOnViewer = true;
        ptp.Commit();

        ProfileSubtypeProperty prop = pspm.Create(ptp);
        prop.DefaultPrivacy = Privacy.Public;
        prop.IsUserEditable = true;
        prop.PrivacyPolicy = PrivacyPolicy.OptIn;
        prop.UserOverridePrivacy = true;
        pspm.Add(prop);
        }
        catch (Exception exception)
        {
        Debug.Write(exception.Message);
        }
        siteColl.Dispose();
    }
```

The above code will create a property named *MyProperty* of a *string* type. The property will also be visible to the user on their profile page where they can also make the value of the property visible to other users or private

9. Deploy the solution using Visual Studio. You may get an error from Visual Studio complaining about activating our custom feature. The reason behind the error is that the account which Visual Studio uses to activate the feature doesn't have access to the user profile service application. Follow to the next step to resolve this

10. Navigate to the **Central Administration | Manage service applications** | select **User Profile Service Application** | in the ribbon, click **Administrators** button

11. In the windows provided, enter the user you're using to run your site, in our case

administrator and assign this user permission to **Manage Profiles** as shown below:

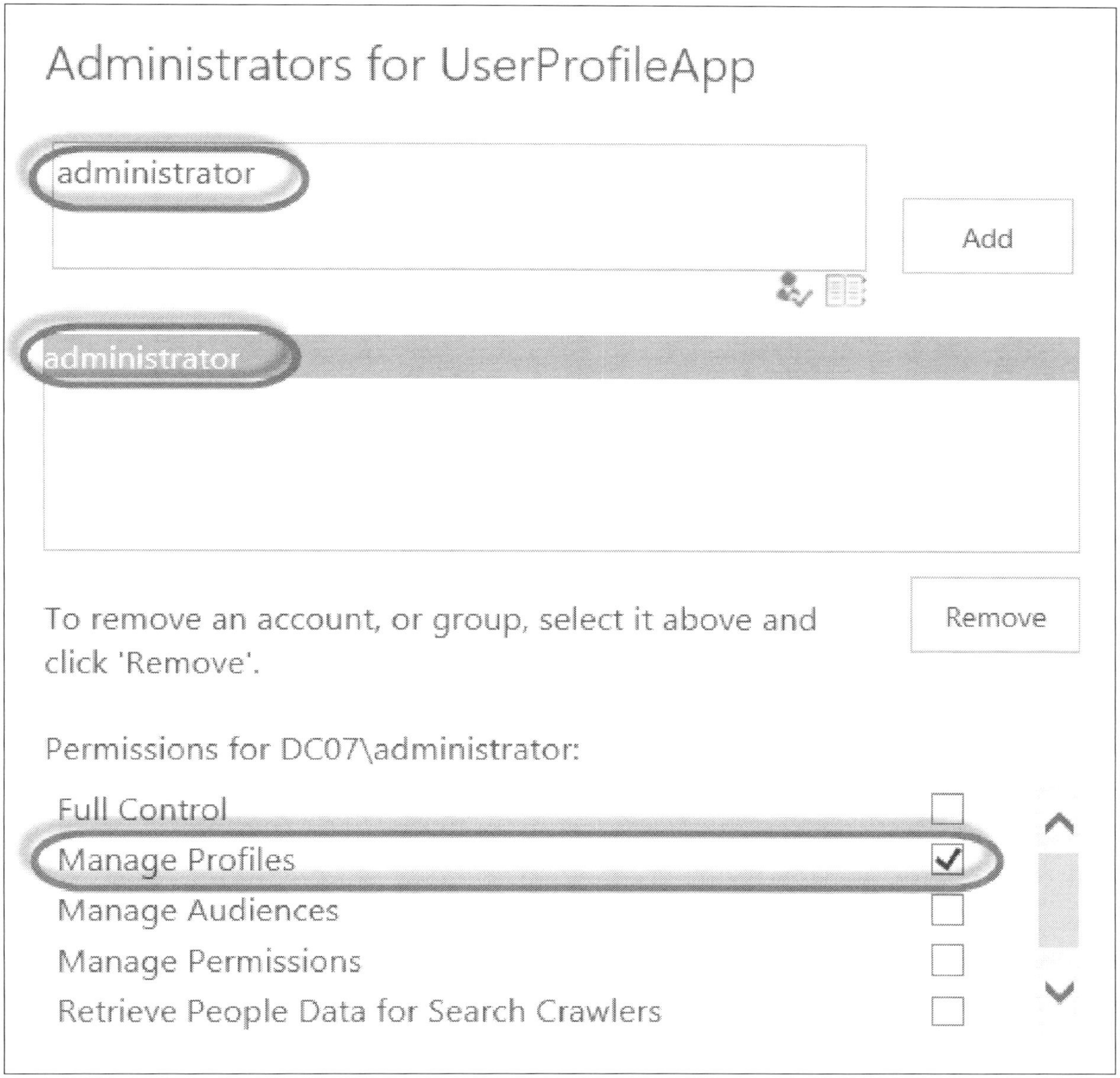

Figure 4.11.2 Adding user profile administrator

12. Click OK

Customizing features of your collaboration solution

13. Now we'll activate already deployed feature right from within SharePoint. Return back to your debug site and click the **Gear Menu** | **Site Settings** | **Site collection features** | locate the feature titled the same name as in our Visual Studio project | click **Activate**

14. Once the feature has activated you will see its status changed to **Active**

15. Click the administrators name to access their **About Me** page as shown below

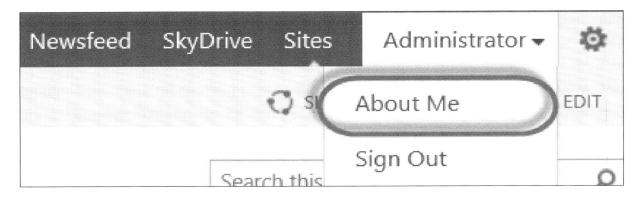

Figure 4.11.3 Accessing user profile properties for the user

16. Click **edit your profile** | from the property groups select **Custom Properties** as shown below

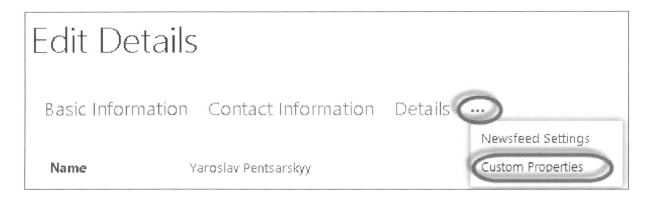

Figure 4.11.4 Accessing custom user profile properties

17. From there you will see our custom property titled *My Property*, where you can enter custom data and save it. Now the information added will be available to out-of-the-box and custom features

Let's now see how we can save and read information from our custom property

Related scenarios

- *Working with user profiles and user profile properties*
- *Using user profile property values in your solution*

Customizing features of your collaboration solution

4.12 Using user profile property values in your solution

Scenario

In the last two scenarios we've looked at how you can create a new user profile and add custom user profile properties to be used by all users. In this scenario we'll combine the knowledge from the previous two to do something very practical – read and write user property values from within your web parts and custom controls. This method is very handy to store user specific preference and render your custom components according to a user preference

Set up

In this scenario, we'll be using the solution from the scenario *Customizing SharePoint 2013 suite bar menu*; we'll be adding code right to it. We'll also assume that you have created a new custom property from the previous scenario *Creating custom user profile properties*.

If you're using the source code provided with this scenario, ensure you change the Site URL in Visual Studio: open the **properties window** (press F4) | select the project name in **solution explorer** | set the **Site URL** to your actual debug URL.

How it's done

1. Open Visual Studio solution we have created in scenario titled *Customizing SharePoint 2013 suite bar menu*

2. Right click on the project name | **Add** | **New Item ...** | select **Visual Web Part**

3. Set the name for the web part to **ConfigureNavigationItem**

4. A New feature will be created to provision the web part, set the name of the feature to **ProvisionWebPart**

5. Add the following assembly reference to your project:

a. Microsoft.Office.Server.UserProfiles.dll

6. Switch into the code view of the newly created web part user control: **ConfigureNavigationItem.ascx** and add the following code to it:

```
Link Title: <asp:textbox runat="server" id="NavTitle"></asp:textbox>
<br/>
Link URL: <asp:textbox runat="server" id="NavUrl"></asp:textbox>
<br/>
<asp:linkbutton runat="server" id="SaveNav" OnClick="SaveNav_Click">Save</asp:linkbutton>
```

The above declares two text boxes to store the name of the link and the URL as well as a button to save the setting

7. Switch into the code view of the web part user control code file: **ConfigureNavigationItem.ascx.cs** and add the following namespace references:

    a. *using Microsoft.SharePoint;*
    b. *using Microsoft.Office.Server.UserProfiles;*

8. Add the following method right below the **Page_Load**:

```
protected void SaveNav_Click(object sender, EventArgs e)
{
string socialDataStatsSite = SPContext.Current.Site.Url;
using (SPSite siteColl = new SPSite(socialDataStatsSite))
{
SPServiceContext serviceContext = SPServiceContext.GetContext(siteColl);
UserProfile userProfile = ProfileLoader.GetProfileLoader().GetUserProfile();
if (userProfile["MyProperty"] != null)
```

```
{
userProfile["MyProperty"].Add(NavTitle.Text + ";" + NavUrl.Text);
userProfile.Commit();
}
}
}
```

The above code will save the values of Title and URL to the user profile property called *MyProperty* which we created earlier. Alternatively, you can use any other string type property in the user profile.

9. Replace the code of **Page_Load** with the following:

```
protected void Page_Load(object sender, EventArgs e)
{
   string socialDataStatsSite = SPContext.Current.Site.Url;
   using (SPSite siteColl = new SPSite(socialDataStatsSite))
   {
      SPServiceContext serviceContext = SPServiceContext.GetContext(siteColl);
      UserProfile userProfile = ProfileLoader.GetProfileLoader().GetUserProfile();
      if (userProfile["MyProperty"] != null
         && userProfile["MyProperty"].Value !=null)
      {
         string propValue = userProfile["MyProperty"].Value.ToString();
         string[] navValues = propValue.Split(';');
         NavTitle.Text = navValues[0];
         NavUrl.Text = navValues[1];
      }
   }
```

}

The above code will load the values from the *MyProperty* into our text boxes representing the Title and the URL

10. Now that the values should have been stored in the user profile property, we can load them in our **UserControl1.ascx.cs** representing our custom suite bar. There we will load the values and render a new link. Add the following namespace references in the **UserControl1.ascx.cs** to allow us to work with user profile service application:

    a. *using Microsoft.SharePoint;*
    b. *using Microsoft.Office.Server.UserProfiles;*

11. Replace the code of the **Render** method with the following:

```
protected override void Render(HtmlTextWriter writer)
{
   string socialDataStatsSite = SPContext.Current.Site.Url;
   using (SPSite siteColl = new SPSite(socialDataStatsSite))
   {
   SPServiceContext serviceContext = SPServiceContext.GetContext(siteColl);
   UserProfile userProfile = ProfileLoader.GetProfileLoader().GetUserProfile();
   if (userProfile[PropertyConstants.AboutMe] != null
   && userProfile[PropertyConstants.AboutMe].Value != null)
   {
   string propValue = userProfile["MyProperty"].Value.ToString();
   string[] navValues = propValue.Split(';');
   writer.RenderBeginTag(HtmlTextWriterTag.Style);
   writer.Write(".ms-core-suiteLinkList {display: inline-block;}");
   writer.RenderEndTag();
```

Customizing features of your collaboration solution

```
writer.AddAttribute(HtmlTextWriterAttribute.Class, "ms-core-
suiteLinkList");
writer.RenderBeginTag(HtmlTextWriterTag.Ul);
RenderSuiteLink(writer, navValues[1], navValues[0], navValues[0]+"
Link", false);
writer.RenderEndTag();
    }
  }
  base.Render(writer);
}
```

The above code has been modified from the original version we had in order to retrieve only the available profile property values and make them into a links in our suite bar

12. Deploy the solution with Visual Studio and access the debug URL

13. Edit the landing page and add our newly provisioned configuration web part from the **Custom** web part category | **ConfigureNavigationItem** | save the page

14. The two text boxes are empty since no information has been loaded into the user profile; enter the title and the URL for the desired link and hit the **Save** link

15. When the page refreshes, you should see your newly added link in the suite bar

Related scenarios

- *Working with user profiles and user profile properties*
- *Creating custom user profile properties*
- *Customizing SharePoint 2013 suite bar menu*

4.13 Creating recurring background running processes using SharePoint timer jobs

Scenario

SharePoint has quite a few out-of-the-box timer jobs performing various functions within the platform. Timer jobs are custom .NET code running within a context of SharePoint, meaning that you have access to the SharePoint object model. Also, administrators will have access to the interface where they can change the schedule and the frequency of the timer job. Typically you would create a timer job when the operation just takes too long to perform and must be executed in the background and save the results for later. Also, you would create a timer job to perform repetitive tasks and constantly update results. An example could be parsing all of the pages on the site building the list of most accessed pages and presenting it to the user. This activity is definitely going to take time and the rank will change over time, so a scenario like this would call for a timer job.

Set up

Since this scenario isn't specific to a type of a site we're using, we'll be deploying and testing our job on our existing team site at URL *http://sp2013*. If you're using the source code provided with this scenario, ensure you change the Site URL in Visual Studio: open the **properties window** (press F4) | select the project name in **solution explorer** | set the **Site URL** to your actual debug URL.

Before we begin

Let's first take a look at where in SharePoint you can see all of the out-of-the-box and custom timer job definitions as well as where to change their schedule and frequency.

1. Navigate to the **Central Administration**

2. Select the **Monitoring** link of the left part of your side bar | under **Time Jobs** category | click **Review job definitions**

3. The list of timer job definitions you will see represent an instance of the timer job

Customizing features of your collaboration solution

running. You will also see which web application is the particular job running and the schedule at which it's running

4. To see the details of the timer job schedule and to change the schedule or frequency click on one of the job definitions. From here you can also force a one time run of the timer job, which is frequently used for testing

Just as many other components in SharePoint, your time job will be provisioned using a feature.

Let's go ahead to see how we create one next.

How it's done

1. Create new Visual Studio **SharePoint 2013 Empty Project**

2. Specify *http://sp2013* as your debug URL and choose **Deploy as a farm solution** option

3. In the solution explorer, right click on the folder named **Features | Add Feature**

4. Set **ProvisionTimerJob** as the name for your feature and set its scope to **WebApplication**. That's right, your timer jobs can only be deployed to a web application and are available to all of the sites using that web application

5. Add a new event receiver to a feature and switch to its code file : **ProvisionTimerJob.EventReceiver.cs**

6. Add the following namespace references to the receiver code:

    a. *using Microsoft.SharePoint.Administration;*
    b. *using System.Diagnostics;*

7. Replace the **FeatureActivated** method of the receiver with the following code:

    ```
    public override void FeatureActivated(SPFeatureReceiverProperties properties)
    ```

```csharp
{
    SPWebApplication webApplication = (SPWebApplication)properties.
    Feature.Parent;
    SPJobDefinition jobDefinition = webApplication.JobDefinitions["My
    Timer Job"];
    if (jobDefinition != null)
    {
    jobDefinition.Delete();
    }
    try
    {
    MyJobDefinition myJobDefinition = new MyJobDefinition("MyTimerJobID",
    webApplication);
    SPMinuteSchedule minuteSchedule = new SPMinuteSchedule();
    minuteSchedule.BeginSecond = 1;
    minuteSchedule.EndSecond = 59;
    minuteSchedule.Interval = 1;
    myJobDefinition.Schedule = minuteSchedule;
    myJobDefinition.Update();
    }
    catch (Exception ex)
    {
    Debug.Write("Exception in Feature Activated occurred: " +
    ex.Message);
    }
}
```

The above code will check whether an existing instance of a timer job already exists and will delete it first. Then, we provision a new instance of a timer job and give it an initial schedule to run every 1 minute, which is quite frequent for a timer job and you wouldn't want to run complex operations every minute in your production

Customizing features of your collaboration solution

environment.

8. Next, we'll delete our timer job when the feature is deactivated. Replace the **FeatureDeactivating** method of the receiver with the following code:

```
public override void FeatureDeactivating(SPFeatureReceiverProperties properties)
{
   SPWebApplication webApplication =
   (SPWebApplication)properties.Feature.Parent;
   SPJobDefinition jobDefinition =
   webApplication.JobDefinitions["My Timer Job"];
   if (jobDefinition != null)
   {
   jobDefinition.Delete();
   }
}
```

Above code deletes an existing timer job definition

9. You may have noticed that in **FeatureActivated** we reference a class called **MyJobDefinition**, this is the class which runs main timer job logic. Let's create a new class in Visual Studio by adding new item to the solution structure, right click SharePoint project name | **Add** | **New Item ...** | from **Code** category | select **Class** | set the file name to **MyJobDefinition.cs** | click **Add**

10. Add the following namespace references to the newly created class:

    a. *using Microsoft.SharePoint.Administration;*
    b. *using System.Diagnostics;*

11. Replace the default definition of the class with the following code:

```
public class MyJobDefinition : SPJobDefinition
{
```

```csharp
public MyJobDefinition()
: base()
{
}
public MyJobDefinition(string jobName, SPWebApplication
webApplication)
: base(jobName, webApplication, null, SPJobLockType.Job)
{
this.Title = "My Timer Job Title";
}
public override void Execute(Guid targetInstanceId)
{
try
{
SPWebApplication webApplication = this.Parent as SPWebApplication;
// TODO: your custom execution goes here
}
catch (Exception ex)
{
Debug.Write("Problem during service job execution:" + ex.Message);
}
}
}
```

Above our class will have only one method, **Execute**, performing the execution of the custom code that will run as a part of the scheduled process. Currently our **Execute** method is empty, so our timer job will run and not perform any action. The goal is to get you familiar with the framework of timer job

12. Deploy the solution using Visual Studio

13. Navigate to the **Central Administration**

Customizing features of your collaboration solution

14. Select **Monitoring** link of the left part of your side bar | under **Time Jobs** category | click **Review job definitions**

15. Locate the item with the title *My Timer Job Title*, that's our timer job. If you have more than one web application installed in the farm you will notice two timer job instances; one for each web application. The **FeatureActivated** method provisioning the timer job will activate the feature at each web application, so if you like to isolate the timer job only to a specific web application you may perform a check on the name of the web application in **FeatureActivated** method before adding a timer job to that web application

16. Click on the item to see details about timer job schedule

Since timer job logic is .NET code, let's see how you can debug it. We've looked at debugging of .NET code inside custom web parts and event receivers. Debugging the timer job is a tiny bit different because they run as a part of the **SharePoint Timer Service** process:

1. In Visual Studio, locate the **Execute** method inside **MyJobDefinition.cs** class and place a breakpoint at the beginning of the **Execute**

2. From the Visual Studio **Debug** menu select **Attach to Process**

3. From the list of available processes, select **OWSTIMER.exe**. Note that you may have to select **Show processes from all users** and **Show processes in all sessions** to see the **OWSTIMER.exe** in the list

4. Once ready, click **Attach** and wait for the time job to trigger. Once the time job has triggered according to your schedule, you will be taken to the Visual Studio breakpoint you have selected. Alternatively you can force triggering of the timer job from Central Administration

Related scenarios

- *Debugging your SharePoint solution*

4.14 Defining content expiration and automating provisioning of out-of-the-box workflows

Scenario

When building collaboration solution, it's not just about lists and calendars, etc; people store documents on the site, lots of them. Over time those documents become old and irrelevant and new versions confuse users who are looking for information in search results or site hierarchy. SharePoint 2013 has a solution to manage expired content and help content authors archive or delete irrelevant documents. In this scenario we'll use out-of-the-box document retention and expiration policies along with workflows to automatically remind users of expiring content and delete the content if it's past the expiration threshold.

Set up

Since this scenario isn't specific to a type of a site we're using, we'll be deploying and testing our solution on our existing team site at URL *http://sp2013*. If you're using the source code provided with this scenario, ensure you change the Site URL in Visual Studio: open the **properties window** (press F4) | select the project name in **solution explorer** | set the **Site URL** to your actual debug URL.

Before we begin

First, let's take a look at out-of-the-box user interface available in SharePoint 2013 to manage content in libraries. Assuming you're logged in to the site with at least one document library, navigate to that library:

1. From the ribbon, select the **Library** tab | click the **Workflow Settings** fly out menu | select **Add a Workflow**

2. From the list of available workflows, you can see **Disposition Approval** with the following description: *Manages document expiration and retention by allowing participants to decide whether to retain or delete expired documents*. We'll use this workflow to ensure authors knows that their documents are approaching expiration date set by a company

Customizing features of your collaboration solution

3. Give a workflow instance a name, such as *DispositionReminder*

4. From the **Start Options**, notice the check box: *Creating a new item will start this workflow*. This will trigger the workflow immediately on item document creation or upload; we don't want immediate notification, only after a certain period of time

5. Click **OK** to add a workflow

Now let's set up an expiration rule to trigger this workflow in 60 days:

1. Navigate back to the same document library view as before, from the ribbon, select the **Library** tab | click the **Library Settings** button

2. On the following page click the link: **Information management policy settings**, located under **Permissions and management**

3. Since policies apply not only to libraries but also to a specific type of content, click **Document** content type to ensure our policy is applied only to files of type **Document**

4. Under the **Retention** group | click **Enable Retention** | click **Add a retention stage ...**

5. In the popup, under the **Event** section, you get to pick what will trigger the retention process, let's select the **Created** date + 60 days

6. Next we get to define action, let's pick **Start a workflow**, our newly added workflow will automatically show up in the list

7. Click **OK**

8. Click **Add a retention stage ...** again to add another retention stage

9. This time, we'll select **Created** date + 90 days

10. For the Action, we'll pick **Move to Recycle Bin**

11. Click **OK**

The above will configure for all content of type **Document** in this library to be sent to author for archiving consideration after 60 days or be deleted after 90 days.

Chapter 4

Now let's take a look at how we can automate the provisioning of this policy to the entire group of sites and libraries.

How it's done

1. Create a new Visual Studio **SharePoint 2013 Empty Project**

2. Specify *http://sp2013* as your debug URL and choose **Deploy as a farm solution** option

3. In the solution explorer, right click on the folder named **Features | Add Feature**

4. Set **ProvisionRetentionPolicy** as the name for your feature and set its scope to **Site**

5. Add a new event receiver to a feature and switch to its code file : **ProvisionRetentionPolicy.EventReceiver.cs**

6. Add the following assembly reference to your project:

    a. *Microsoft.Office.Policy.dll*

7. Add the following namespace references to the receiver code:

    a. *using Microsoft.Office.RecordsManagement.InformationPolicy;*
    b. *using Microsoft.SharePoint.Workflow;*
    c. *using System.Globalization;*

8. Replace the **FeatureActivated** method of the receiver with the following code:

```
public override void FeatureActivated(SPFeatureReceiverProperties properties)
{
   SPSite site = properties.Feature.Parent as SPSite;

   // enabling policy feature pre-requisite
   // Features/LocationBasedPolicy
```

Customizing features of your collaboration solution

```csharp
if (site.Features[new Guid("063C26FA-3CCC-4180-8A84-
B6F98E991DF3")]== null)
{
site.Features.Add(new Guid("063C26FA-3CCC-4180-8A84-
B6F98E991DF3"));
}

// enabling out-of-the-box workflows
// Features/Workflows
if (site.Features[new Guid("0AF5989A-3AEA-4519-8AB0-
85D91ABE39FF")] == null)
{
site.Features.Add(new Guid("0AF5989A-3AEA-4519-8AB0-
85D91ABE39FF"));
}

 // iterating through all of the libraries on the site and its sub
sites
foreach (SPWeb web in site.AllWebs)
{
foreach (SPList list in web.Lists)
{
if (list.BaseTemplate == SPListTemplateType.DocumentLibrary)
{
ProvisionApprovalWorkflow(web, list);
CreateExpirationPolicy(list);
}
web.Dispose();
}
}
```

```
      site.Dispose();
  }
```

Above, we start by ensuring some of the mandatory features are active on the site: Policy Feature and Workflows feature. Then we iterate through each sub site on the site collection and each list on the sub site. For each list we make sure that its parent type is document library; after all we don't want to provision policies on other types of lists. Then we can create two custom methods: *ProvisionApprovalWorkflow* will provision disposition approval workflow to the library, and *CreateExpirationPolicy* will create a 2 stage expiration policy. Let's add those methods next

9. Add the following method below the **FeatureActivated**:

```
private static void ProvisionApprovalWorkflow(SPWeb web, SPList list)
{
  // get all workflow templates on site
  SPWorkflowTemplateCollection workflowTemplates = web.
  WorkflowTemplates;

  // get workflow template for disposition approval
  SPWorkflowTemplate workflowTemplate =
  workflowTemplates.GetTemplateByName("Disposition Approval",
  CultureInfo.InvariantCulture);

  // create required lists for workflow tasks and workflow history
  if (web.Lists["Workflow Tasks"]==null)
  {
  web.Lists.Add("Workflow Tasks", string.Empty, SPListTemplateType.
  Tasks);
  }
  if (web.Lists["Workflow History"] == null)
  {
```

Customizing features of your collaboration solution

```
        web.Lists.Add("Workflow History", string.Empty, SPListTemplateType.
        WorkflowHistory);
        }

        // check if workflo already exists on this list
        SPWorkflowAssociation workflowAssociation =
        list.WorkflowAssociations.GetAssociationByName("DispositionRemind
        er", CultureInfo.InvariantCulture);

        if (workflowAssociation != null)
        {
        // add a disposition workflow to a list
        workflowAssociation = SPWorkflowAssociation.CreateListAssociation(wo
        rkflowTemplate,
        "DispositionReminder", web.Lists["Workflow Tasks"], web.
        Lists["Workflow History"]);
        list.WorkflowAssociations.Add(workflowAssociation);
        }
    }
```

The above code will get a hold of the out-of-the-box *Disposition Approval* workflow template and create an instance of it in our library. Since each workflow requires a Task and History list to track progress, we provision those lists unless they have been already created on the site, which is likely if you're provisioning 2 or more workflows on the same site. Next, we'll use those workflows in our policy, provisioned in the method right below

10. Add the following method below the **ProvisionApprovalWorkflow**:

```
    private static void CreateExpirationPolicy(SPList list)
    {
       // get policies for list
```

```csharp
ListPolicySettings listPolicy = new ListPolicySettings(list);

// ensure usage of policy is turned on
if (!listPolicy.ListHasPolicy)
{
listPolicy.UseListPolicy = true;
listPolicy.Update();
}

// policy will be applied on a "Document" content type
SPContentType contentType = list.ContentTypes["Document"];

if (contentType != null)
{
// creating a new policy on the content type
Policy.CreatePolicy(contentType, null);
Policy newPolicy = Policy.GetPolicy(contentType);

// adding policy rule from the resource file
newPolicy.Items.Add("Microsoft.Office.RecordsManagement.
PolicyFeatures.Expiration",
string.Format(Resource1.PolicyRule,
list.WorkflowAssociations.GetAssociationByName("DispositionRemind
er", CultureInfo.InvariantCulture).Id));

// saving changes
newPolicy.Update();
list.Update();
}
}
```

In this code, we ensure the policy is enabled on the list and create a new policy on the *Document* content type. This means that if you have content of different content types, only content inheriting from *Document* out-of-the-box content type will be a subject to our policy. Our policy isn't explicitly defined here since it's an XML markup and we'll keep it separate to ensure our feature receiver code is clean

11. Right click on the Visual Studio project name | **Add** | **New Item ...** | pick **General** category | select **Resource File** | leave the default name of the file and click **Add**

12. In the resource editor click **Add Resource** dropdown | select **Add New Text File** | set a name as **PolicyRule.txt** | click **Add**

13. Add below to the contents of the file :

```xml
<Schedules nextStageId="1" default="false">
<Schedule type="Default">
<stages>
    <data stageId="1">
        <formula id="Microsoft.Office.RecordsManagement.PolicyFeatures.Expiration.Formula.BuiltIn">
        <number>60</number>
        <property>Created</property>
        <propertyId>8c06beca-0777-48f7-91c7-6da68bc07b69</propertyId>
        <period>days</period>
        </formula>
        <action type="workflow" id="{0}"/>
    </data>
    <data stageId="2">
        <formula id="Microsoft.Office.RecordsManagement.PolicyFeatures.Expiration.Formula.BuiltIn">
        <number>90</number>
        <property>Created</property>
```

```xml
            <propertyId>8c06beca-0777-48f7-91c7-6da68bc07b69</propertyId>
            <period>days</period>
            </formula>
            <action type="action" id="Microsoft.Office.RecordsManagement.PolicyFeatures.Expiration.Action.MoveToRecycleBin"/>
        </data>
</stages>
</Schedule>
</Schedules>
```

The above XML is the core of the policy definition. We have 2 stages here marked as *stageId = 1* and *stageId = 2*. First stage activates after 60 days after the *file created date* represented by the field Id for the *created date* in SharePoint. Second stage activates after 90 days of the *created date*. First stage kicks off our workflow assuming it's already added to the library. Whether there has been an action from a user or not, after 90 days we move the document to the SharePoint recycle bin

14. Deploy the solution using Visual Studio and verify that all of the components and configuration we have gone through in the *Details and notes* section are equally configured

4.15 Getting started with building SharePoint 2013 apps

Scenario

SharePoint 2013 apps are a new concept to implement customizations for SharePoint 2013. Apps are not a replacement for existing customization constructs such as web parts, event receivers, etc. Apps for SharePoint are similar in functionality and concept to many other apps available on a variety of other platforms. It's important to understand the concept of apps and which customization will live up to the feasibility of an app. One of the biggest advantages to apps as opposed to other artifacts is that apps can be distributed through a SharePoint Online Store and made available for a fee (with optional trial period), or free to many users out there. Another advantage to apps is that they can be shared across other Office applications since they're developed with client side code only. Naturally not all of the functionality can be shared since Microsoft Word has its own set of functions not available in SharePoint, but general functionality can be shared.

We won't cover app development in details since it's a separate subject deserving more attention than the scope of this book; however, apps can be important extensibility points to your collaboration solution so we'll cover basics and framework capabilities.

Before we begin

An app is a construct in SharePoint 2013 which utilizes SharePoint 2013 app engine and allows customizations to be packaged and installed from:

- **Corporate catalog** - a private app store available only to users from within your organization
- **Online catalog** – a publically available app store allowing everyone to download your app to their site

In the scenario with private apps, things are much like web parts, they are trusted and the app distributor is likely a known entity to your organization. In case of publically available apps, you can rely on the folks who review incoming apps to make sure they're safe. Also, your apps will be rated by online store users. Additionally your app runs within a safe context and app framework which has quite a few limitations in comparison to web parts for example. For a developer comparison between apps and web parts see my YouTube video titled *SharePoint 2013 apps versus webparts for developers*.

To build apps in this scenario we'll be using a **Developer Site** available from Office 365. The developer site is a special site template which has all the features and configuration allowing developers to start building an app site. Because we're using the Office 365 developer site, you will have the entire configuration taken care of and you can jump right into the developing of your apps without worry.

Because Microsoft wanted to make the development of apps as easy as possible, you can start the development from Visual Studio or right from a web based developer app called Napa. Napa is already installed with Office 365 developer site as an app; yes it's an app to build apps. You can export the project created in Napa to Visual Studio at any time. You can also start with the Visual Studio App template right away without a need for the Napa app.

Apps run no server side code and essentially use JavaScript, HTML, and CSS. JavaScript can execute remote web service calls and if permitted by the user, access SharePoint 2013 server objects, exposed by the API.

An app can have an App Part, which can be inserted using the same user interface as you use when insert web parts. An app part is an iframe running on the page and you can not access other elements on the page from within that iframe. An app part is essentially a **tile** if translated to the concept of apps in Windows Phone or Windows 8. So treat it as a tile, meaning, add only logic showing the status of your app or quick links. In other words, don't make an App Part too busy. The content of an app part can come from another server not even hosted on SharePoint

Each app also gets a web dedicated to hosting any lists needed by the app and a page representing a more ***immersive app experience***. This ***immersive*** page is essentially a page running a full screen version of an app and its content can come from anywhere or directly from SharePoint.

What can be done by an app is limited and restricted by the app framework; if your app requires some significant level of access (for example **write** permission), you can request this access and user can chose whether to grant it or not at the time of app install. We'll see all that in action just below.

Customizing features of your collaboration solution

Set up

In this scenario we'll be using the Office 365 Developer site to get started with building apps. To sign up for an Office 365 Developer Site, search MSDN the following *Sign up for an Office 365 Developer Site*. Follow the instructions to provision your own developer site.

How it's done

1. Navigate to the root of your new developer site:

   https://[your developer site]/SitePages/DevHome.aspx

2. Click **Build an App** button on the main page of the site. You will be redirected to the Napa app

3. Click **Add New Project**

4. From the following dialog, select **App for SharePoint** and for the project name set SPApp and click **Create**

5. You will be presented with an empty project similar to screenshot below:

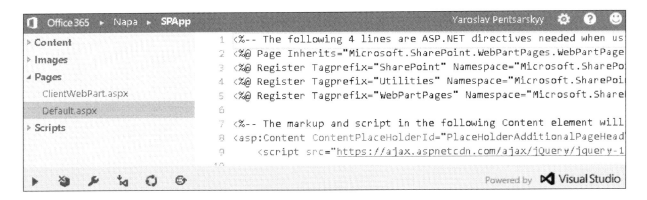

Figure 4.15.1 Napa app development environment

In here, our solution explorer is on the left hand side with the following nodes available:

   a. Content – will contain style sheets. To reference newly added style sheets in your pages use the following convention:

```
<link rel="Stylesheet" type="text/css" href="../Content/NewStyle.css" />
```

b. Images – contains images including app icon used to represent your app in the store

c. Pages – **Default.aspx** is the page representing *immersive* experience for the app and **ClientWebPart.aspx** is the app part content

d. Scripts – contains scripts. Default **App.js** is loaded with a sample code and referenced by default in the **Default.aspx**

You can also add/remove new folders/files within main solution items by right clicking the existing solution folder

6. Select **ClientWebPart.aspx** and insert the following code at the bottom of the `<head>` section:

```
<script src="https://ajax.aspnetcdn.com/ajax/jQuery/jquery-1.6.2.min.js" type="text/javascript"></script>
```

This is a jQuery reference which we actually took from **Default.aspx**

7. Below in the code, replace the content of the <span class="partContent"> with the following code:

```
<span class="partContent">
<a href="#" onclick="$('.partContent').html('Changed label');">Click me</a>
</span>
```

This is a link with a jQuery code command executing on click. When clicked, the link will be replaced with another text

8. Switch to the **Content** project item | select **App.css**. To adjust colors in our app,

match the content of the CSS with the following:

```css
.partDiv
{
    margin: 0;
    padding: 0;
    border: 0;
    position: relative;
    width: 300px;
    height: 200px;
    background-color: #0000FF;
    font-family: 'Segoe UI', Arial, Helvetica, sans-serif;
    font-size: 14pt;
}

.partContent
{
    position: absolute;
    top: 5px;
    left: 5px;
    background-color:#FFFFFF;
}
```

9. Switch to **Scripts/ App.js** and replace the content of the **getUserName()** with the following

```js
function getUserName() {
    user = web.get_currentUser();
    context.load(user);
    context.load(web);
    context.executeQueryAsync(onGetUserNameSuccess,
```

```
onGetUserNameFail);
}
```

Here we'll load the **web** object so its properties are accessible to us

10. Replace the **onGetUserNameSuccess()** with the code below:

```
function onGetUserNameSuccess() {

    $('#message').html('Current user: ' + user.get_title() +

    '<br/>Current web title: ' +web.get_title() +

    '<br/>Current web URL: ' +web.get_url());

}
```

Here we just display the current web title and URL along with the user's name that is currently logged in

11. Click **Run Project** at the bottom of the Napa app and wait for the popup window to open up with your app running in it. Napa will redirect you to the full app page with the details of the current web and user. Notice that the current web context is the web dedicated to an app. This is important to know since you might be expecting for the current context to be a root site context. It's not, it's the context of where the app is installed; and for SharePoint hosted apps it's the dedicated web

12. Navigate back to our root site ***https://[your developer site]/SitePages/DevHome.aspx***

13. Edit the page and select a zone to add a new app part | from the ribbon select **Insert** tab | click the **App Part** button

14. From the list of available app parts pick **SPApp** click **Add**

15. Save the page. You will notice an app part, aka tile of an app, showing on the page. The styles here are defined from **App.css**

16. Click the **Click me** button to see the text in the app part change

Customizing features of your collaboration solution

17. Switch back to Napa and let's take a look at some of the project properties available by clicking the **Properties** button in the bottom left hand corner:

    a. **General | Title** – title of the app
    b. **General | Name** – app name
    c. **General | Icon** – app icon available when the app is installed and in the store
    d. **General** | Start Page – start page for the pull app, any project pages will do
    e. **General | URL Parameters** – by default those are standard tokens, you can specify your own custom parameters, which is a topic for a separate discussion outside of the scope for this book
    f. **Client Web Part | Page** – page dedicated to a app part experience
    g. **Client Web Part | URL Parameters** – same as above
    h. **Client Web Part | Description** – app description which will show up when users choose to add an app part
    i. **Permissions | Content** – app part will request, and it's up to user to grant permission to Read/Write/Manage/Full Control Tenants, Sites, Webs, and Lists
    j. **Permissions | Services** – app part may request Read rights to Search and BCS services and Read/Write to taxonomy service application
    k. **Permissions | Social** – Read/Write/Manage/Full Control to user profiles; Core Social, representing the following; Microfeed, representing posts and activities
    l. **Permissions | Project** – App can request access to additional service applications such as Project Server, Project resources, Reports and Workflows
    m. **Remote Endpoints** | app can request access to remote end points using this interface

18. From the bottom left hand corner click the **Open in Visual Studio** button to open the project from Visual Studio. You will need to choose a language and the project will open

19. From Visual Studio you will see modules representing project items and files within them. You can add new project items here as you see fit. When ready, right click on the **project name** | select **Publish** | select **Finish**. To collect your packaged app, download the ***.app** file

CHAPTER 5

Automating the deployment and configuration of your SharePoint solution

In this chapter:

- Automating SharePoint site provisioning and configuration

5.1 Automating SharePoint site provisioning and configuration

Scenario

Earlier in this book we have already taken a look at how you can automate solution provisioning and activate features on pre-created site collections. In this scenario we'll take our solution a bit further and provision our site structure according to specification; we'll also install solutions and activate any relevant features along the way.

We'll be creating a solution structure according to the following information architecture we looked at earlier:

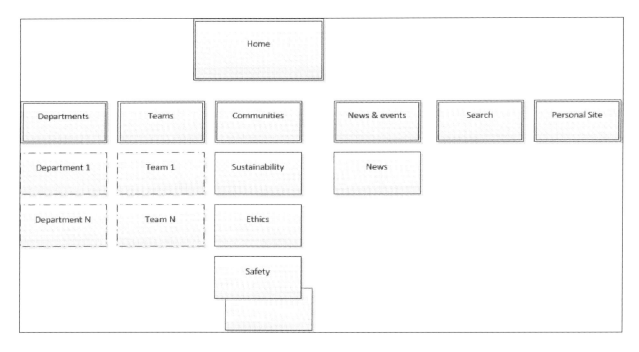

Figure 5.1.1 Example site information architecture

Before we begin

The following set of sites will be created grouped by type of the template they're using:

- Publishing Site

    o Home - root site
    o News and events – sub site of the root

- Enterprise WIKI

    o Departments landing site – sub site of the root
    o Teams landing site – sub site of the root
    o Communities landing site – sub site of the root

- Team Site

    o Department sites – sub site of the Departments landing site
    o Team sites – sub site of the Teams landing site

- Community Site

    o Sustainability – sub site of the Communities landing site
    o Ethics – sub site of the Communities landing site
    o Safety – sub site of the Communities landing site

- Search Site

    o Search – independent site collection parallel to a root

Since the Personal Site requires a bit more configuration, we'll assume it's created manually and not part of our automation script.

All of our sites, except the search site, are sub sites of the root and not independent site collections. If you require more independence for, say team sites, you may choose them to be individual site collections and create them using the same method as the search site. Some site templates require additional features activated before they can run; community site is an example. The community site requires the **SocialSite** feature activated on the site collection level. Since our community sites are children of the root site collection, the dependent **SocialSite** feature, will have to be activated at the root level in order for the site

Automating the deployment and configuration of your SharePoint solution

to be created. In your scenario, you may run into the same requirements where you need to activate site collection features at the parent site collection to make sure child sites can be created.

Also, you will notice that the script below will have a placeholder for you to provision your custom solutions just as we did in scenario: *Putting it all together: automated installation of your branding package to multiple environments*. In our case we won't be provisioning any custom solutions but if we were, you can place the corresponding WSP file in the same directory as our script to install it. You will also need to toggle the **Deploy** attribute in the **Solutions** node of the configuration file to **True** to ensure the solutions are deployed.

It's important to mention that the script we'll be looking at below will delete and recreate any of the site collections you have defined in the script if they already exist. Beware of this since you will loose data you have already created on those sites with same URL

How it's done

1. Download and extract the source code accompanying this scenario. The source code represents a PowerShell script used to deploy set of site collections and sub sites as well as activate their features

2. Open the **Config.xml** from the package using Visual Studio or Notepad++; the resulting configuration file should look similar to below:

```xml
<?xml version="1.0" encoding="utf-8"?>

<Setup WebAppUrl="http://sp2013srv">
<Solutions Deploy="false">
<Solution WebApplication="False">CustomSolution.wsp</Solution>
</Solutions>


<SiteCollections Deploy="true">
<SiteCollection Name="Home" Url="/" OwnerAlias="Domain\Administrator" Template="BLANKINTERNET#0">
```

```xml
<Features>
<Feature Id="4326E7FC-F35A-4b0f-927C-36264B0A4CF0"
Name="SocialSite"></Feature>
</Features>
<Web Name="Departments" Url="/Departments" Template="ENTERWIKI#0">
<Web Name="Department1" Url="/Department1" Template="STS#1">
</Web>
<Web Name="Department2" Url="/Department2" Template="STS#1">
</Web>
</Web>
<Web Name="Teams" Url="/Teams" Template="ENTERWIKI#0">
<Web Name="Team1" Url="/Team1" Template="STS#1">
    <!--Features>
        <Feature Id="" Name=""></Feature>
    </Features-->
</Web>
<Web Name="Team2" Url="/Team2" Template="STS#1">
    <!--Features>
        <Feature Id="" Name=""></Feature>
    </Features-->
</Web>
</Web>
<Web Name="Communities" Url="/Communities" Template="ENTERWIKI#0">
<Web Name="Sustainability" Url="/Sustainability"
Template="COMMUNITY#0">
</Web>
<Web Name="Ethics" Url="/Ethics" Template="COMMUNITY#0">
</Web>
<Web Name="Safety" Url="/Safety" Template="COMMUNITY#0">
</Web>
```

Automating the deployment and configuration of your SharePoint solution

```
</Web>
<Web Name="News and Events" Url="/NewsAndEvents"
Template="BLANKINTERNET#0">
</Web>
</SiteCollection>
<SiteCollection Name="Search" Url="/search" OwnerAlias="Domain\
Administrator" Template="SRCHCEN#0">
</SiteCollection>
</SiteCollections>
</Setup>
```

3. Ensure the following values reflect the configuration of your environment:

    a. **WebAppUrl** – set to the URL of your SharePoint web application

    b. **Solutions** node | **Deploy** attribute – defines whether custom solutions listed just below will be deployed or not

    c. **Solutions** node | **Solution** nodes – define any custom solutions, if any, to be deployed as a part of this script. The name within the solution is the WSP file which must be located in the same directory as this script

    d. **Solution** node | **WebApplication** attribute - is set to **True** if our custom solution contains any web application resources such as web parts, user controls, etc. To make things simple, leave the value as **False**, and if this setting is incorrect, you will get an error during running of the script at which point you can flip the switch to **True**

    e. **SiteCollections** – is a set of nodes representing each individual site we'll be creating. In our case we have the root site collection, named **Home**, and the search site collection named **Search**

    f. **SiteCollection** node | **Url** attribute – the URL of the site collection. New site collections will be created under the managed path of **sites,** unless different managed path provided, see next item

g. **SiteCollection** node | **ManagedPath** attribute – the **Managed Path** for each site. In our case, it's the default **sites**

h. **Feature** node | **Id** attribute – the value of the specific **Id** for any Feature required to be activated on the site collection. In our case we're activating **SocialSite** feature required by the community sub sites

i. **Feature** node | **Name** attribute – if this is your custom feature, then replace the name to the concatenated value of your Visual Studio project name and the Feature which provisions the master page: **[ProjectName]_ [MasterPageFeatureName]**. This is how Visual Studio names custom features, in our case, however, we're using out of the box feature named simply **SocialSite**. The same convention for features applies to web features

j. **Webs** node | **Web** child node – represents any child webs provisioned under the site collection or parent sites

k. **Web** node | **Name** attribute – similarly to the site collection, this is how we define the name of the sub site

l. **Web** node | **Url** attribute – defines the URL of the site under the site collection or a parent web

m. **Web** node | **Template** – defines the template used for the site providing of course it's all installed on the server

4. Ensure that the username in node **SiteCollection** | attribute **OwnerAlias** is set to the username representing your farm administrator. You only need to provide this setting for the site collection since their sub sites will inherit the setting automatically

5. If you have any custom features you'd like to have activated on any of the sites you can declare them under the **Web** node with the code similar to below:

```
<Web Name="Team1" Url="/Team1" Template="STS#1">
    <Features>
        <Feature Id="[Feature ID]" Name="[Feature Name]"></Feature>
```

```
            </Features>
</Web>
```

The features here can perform any post-site provisioning actions. That's right; unlike features defined in **onet.xml** activating as the site provisions, features installed here will be activated after the site has been provisioned. This might even eliminate the need for you to create custom site templates since you can make many customizations right from within the script

6. Save the configuration file with the desired settings.

    a. Before you run the script, remember that it will delete and recreate any of the site collections you have defined in the script if they already exist. Beware of this since you will loose data you have already created on those sites with same URL

7. When ready run the **SetupSites.bat** to start provisioning your solutions and site collection structure

8. To verify, ensure the script has ran and has not returned any errors. Then you can log into SharePoint and verify that the desired structure has been created according to your defined configuration

Related scenarios

- *Putting it all together: automated installation of your branding package to multiple environments*

etc ...

Here we are ... hopefully you have gotten a good overview and practical tips on what SharePoint 2013 collaboration features are all about and how you can customize your site. If you haven't already, be sure to check out the source code for most chapters at **www.sharemuch.com**, also I try to post regularly on my YouTube channel **ShareMuch**. On my blog, you can also reach me and tell me what you liked and didn't like about the book. I do hope you did find this book resourceful and complete with examples that closely resemble your scenarios, and that everything actually worked from the first time.

If you find this book worth sharing with your peers or colleagues, please do so; you can also make me very happy by posting your review on Amazon. Authors like me read reviews religiously and you won't believe how warm it makes me feel to read a good review about my work.

Thank you!

Yaroslav

Index

Symbols

<s:colorPalette> 78

A

Add a Web Part 18
Add a workflow 34
Add a Workflow 243
Add Event Receiver 133
Alternate CSS 117
Announcements app 32
Application Management 55
App Part 257
Approval and Feedback workflows 34
apps 252
automated installation 151
Automating SharePoint site provisioning 259

B

branding 68
branding package 151
breadcrumb 107

C

Calendar App 30
Central Administration 12
Change the look 76
CloudShare 10
codeplex 69
collaboration site master page 93
collaboration site templates 158
Committee idea site 36
Committee site 27
Community Site 36
Composed looks 76
Contacts app 33
Content Editor 26
Content Editor web part 178
content expiration 243
Content Query Web Part 20
content roll up 183
Content Rollup 20
Content Search 22

Content Search Web Part 22
Content section 73
content type 20
ContentType 172
Content Types 190
Controls 70
cookie 99
Corporate catalog 252
Corporate Processes 49
Correlation ID 198
Create site collections 17
Create Term 52
Crowdsourcing site 36
Customizing list view 186
custom look 76
custom page layouts 119

D

Debug 201
Debugging 197
Department site 27
Deployment Type 173
Design Manager 15
Developer Site 253
development environment 10
diagnostic logging 198
Discussion management 41
Display Templates 24
Documents library 33

E

eature manifest 147
Edit Page 29
Element Manifest 173
Enterprise Search Center 55
Enterprise WIKI 49
events triggering 194
extending a SharePoint master page 97
Extending publishing 165

F

farm solution 93
Features 70

G

GhostableinLibrary 80
Glossary site 49

H

Header 73
"How To" library 49

I

Issue tracking app 33

J

JavaScript 97
job definitions 237
jQuery 97, 100

L

Left Navigation 73
Links app 33
list events 194

List Settings 30
look and feel of Personal Site 135

M

ManagedMetadata 207
Managed Metadata Service Application 51
managed navigation 202
Manage web applications 55
Manuals library 49
Mapped Folder 80
Mapped folders 71
master page 84
Master pages and page layouts 74
MasterUrl 163
Media and Content 26
Moderation 41
Modules 71
My Site Host location 60
My Site Settings 60

N

Newsfeed 61
New Term Set 52

O

onet 199
ONET 163
Online catalog 252

P

page layout 121
Page Layout 18

page layout components 121
page properties 19
Permission Level 60
Personal Site 59, 146
Pictures Web Part 25
Policies and Procedures site 49
Popular Items Web Part 25
Preferred Search Center 60
Project site 27
Project Site 44
Project Summary web part 47
Property Mappings 24
Provisioning content 170
Provisioning web parts 178
PublishingPageLayout 172
Publishing Portal 15
Publishing Site 16

Q

Query Builder 23

R

Recently Changed Items Web Part 25
recurring background running processes 237
Refiner web part 58
Relevant Documents Web Part 25
Reputation Settings 43
Retention 244

S

Script Editor 26
search box 108

Search Box web part 58
Search Navigation web part 58
Search Results web part 58
search site master page 128
Security Trimming 60
SharePoint Server Publishing Infrastructure 50
SharePoint Solution Package 69, 71
Site collection features 50
Site Definition 167
site navigation 15, 32
site templates 14
site template structure 159
spcolor 78
Subsite templates 28
Sub tasks 47
suite bar 108, 214
Survey app 33

T

Tasks app 33
Team Site 27
Team site layout structure 73
Theme 74, 77
Timeline 46
timer jobs 237

U

unique permissions 37
Unique permissions 38
user profile properties 219, 224
user profile property 232

user profiles 219
User Profile Service Application 59

V

Videos Web Part 25
Views 185
virtual machine 10

W

Web Designer Galleries 74
Web Pages Web Part 25
Web part options 29
WebPartOrder 180
WebPartZoneID 180
webtempsps 166
WIKI categories 51
WIKI Categories 54
workflows 243
Workflow Settings 34
Workgroup idea site 36
Workgroup site 27

Made in the USA
Charleston, SC
12 May 2014